ANURAG KUMAR

Unwavering Loyalty: Dogs Who Changed Lives

5 Heartwarming Stories of Canine Devotion and the Bonds That Last Forever

Copyright © 2024 by Anurag Kumar

All rights reserved. No part of this publication may be reproduced, stored or transmitted in any form or by any means, electronic, mechanical, photocopying, recording, scanning, or otherwise without written permission from the publisher. It is illegal to copy this book, post it to a website, or distribute it by any other means without permission.

First edition

This book was professionally typeset on Reedsy. Find out more at reedsy.com

Contents

Introduction: A Love Like No Other	1
Hachiko – The Dog Who Waited Forever	4
Capitan – The Cemetery Guardian	21
Bobbie – The Wonder Dog	39
Greyfriars Bobby – The Skye Terrier Who Stayed	56
Balto – The Sled Dog Who Saved a Town	75
What Dogs Teach Us About Loyalty	93
Conclusion: A Life Inspired by Loyalty	114
Tribute	118

Introduction: A Love Like No Other

Dogs have a way of speaking to our hearts without uttering a single word. Their wagging tails, soulful eyes, and boundless affection remind us daily of the purest form of love. But beyond their playful antics and warm snuggles lies something even more profound: their extraordinary loyalty. It's a devotion that often transcends what we think is possible—a bond so deep that it can inspire stories that are passed down through generations.

Welcome to *Unwavering Loyalty: Dogs Who Changed Lives*. This book is a celebration of that devotion, a tribute to the dogs who have shown us the true meaning of unwavering love. Through five emotional stories, we'll journey into the lives of remarkable canines who proved time and again that loyalty isn't just a trait; it's their very essence.

For centuries, dogs have been humanity's trusted companions. They guard our homes, guide us through challenges, and comfort us in our darkest hours. But what makes their loyalty so unique is that it's given freely, without expectation. A dog doesn't care about your flaws or your failures—they love you for who you are, exactly as you are. And in return, they ask only for your love.

Each chapter in this book explores a different story of a dog's loyalty, from the legendary Hachiko, who waited for his owner at a train station for nearly a decade, to lesser-known but equally inspiring tales of devotion. These stories aren't just about the dogs—they're about the bonds they shared with their humans. They're about the strength of connection, the power of hope, and the beauty of love that defies all odds.

As you read these tales, you'll find yourself laughing, crying, and marveling at the depth of these bonds. You'll see how dogs have changed lives, brought communities together, and even taught us invaluable lessons about ourselves. Because in every wag of the tail, every joyful bark, and every quiet moment of companionship, there's a story waiting to be told—a story of loyalty that knows no bounds.

This book isn't just for dog lovers; it's for anyone who's ever been touched by love, loyalty, and the magic of connection. It's for those who believe in the power of devotion and the beauty of small acts that leave lasting impressions. Whether you've grown up with a furry friend by your side or simply admire dogs from afar, these stories will remind you of the incredible ways they enrich our lives.

So, settle in with your favorite beverage, perhaps with your own four-legged friend curled up beside you. Let these stories warm your heart and inspire your spirit. Through the pages of this book, you'll come to see why dogs truly are our best friends—and why their loyalty is a gift we should cherish always.

Welcome to the journey. Let's celebrate the incredible, unwavering love of dogs together.

INTRODUCTION: A LOVE LIKE NO OTHER

***

Hachiko – The Dog Who Waited Forever

The Professor and His Loyal Friend: How Hachiko's Bond with Professor Ueno Became Legendary

In the bustling city of Tokyo during the early 1920s, a unique friendship blossomed—a bond so pure and steadfast that it would transcend time and borders, touching hearts across generations. This is the story of Hachiko, a humble Akita dog, and his master, Professor Hidesaburo Ueno. Their connection was not just one of companionship but an extraordinary testament to loyalty and love, a tale that would inspire millions around the globe.

A Serendipitous Beginning

Hachiko's journey with Professor Ueno began in 1924 when the professor, a scholar at the prestigious University of Tokyo, decided to adopt a dog. Hachiko, then a fluffy cream-colored Akita puppy, entered Ueno's life as a gift. The professor named him "Hachiko," reflecting the Japanese word for "eighth," symbolizing good fortune and prosperity.

From the very start, Hachiko was more than a pet to Ueno; he was family. Their daily routine quickly became a cherished ritual. Each morning, Hachiko would accompany Ueno to Shibuya Station, tail wagging with excitement as the professor boarded his train to work. In the evening, like clockwork, Hachiko would be there waiting, his expressive eyes scanning the crowd for his beloved master.

An Unbreakable Bond

The relationship between Hachiko and Ueno was marked by quiet moments of companionship and mutual understanding. Hachiko's unwavering devotion brought joy and comfort to the professor's otherwise busy academic life. Neighbors in Shibuya often marveled at the dog's dedication, noticing how he stood vigil at the station entrance, rain or shine, until Ueno returned.

Their bond was one of those rare connections that defy explanation—a profound friendship that transcended the boundaries of species. To Professor Ueno, Hachiko wasn't just a pet but a constant source of unconditional love. For Hachiko, Ueno was his world.

The Tragic Day That Changed Everything

On May 21, 1925, tragedy struck. Professor Ueno suffered a sudden brain hemorrhage while at work and passed away. He never returned to Shibuya Station that evening, leaving Hachiko waiting, confused and heartbroken.

But Hachiko's loyalty was unshaken. The next day, he returned to the station at the usual time, hopeful that his master would emerge from the train as he always had. Day after day, Hachiko continued this ritual, undeterred by the changing seasons or the indifference of the bustling crowds.

Years of Vigilance

Hachiko's daily presence at Shibuya Station soon caught the attention of commuters and local residents. At first, some pitied the dog, while others dismissed him as a stray. However, as the weeks turned into months and months into years, his persistence touched the hearts of those who witnessed his vigil.

Local vendors began to feed Hachiko, and many looked forward to seeing him each day. The dog's story spread, and he became a symbol of unwavering loyalty in Japan. People started referring to him affectionately as "Chuken Hachiko," meaning "Faithful Dog Hachiko."

Despite the years that passed, Hachiko never gave up hope. For nine long years, he continued to wait for Professor Ueno, his devotion never wavering.

A Nation Inspired

Hachiko's story gained national attention when a journalist wrote an article about him in 1932. The piece highlighted the dog's extraordinary loyalty and moved readers across Japan. Hachiko quickly became a cultural icon, embodying the values of fidelity and perseverance that are deeply revered in Japanese society.

The Akita breed, once relatively unknown, gained popularity due to Hachiko's fame. His story even reached schoolchildren, who learned about his loyalty in their textbooks.

In 1934, a bronze statue of Hachiko was erected at Shibuya Station, with the faithful dog himself present at the unveiling. It was a moment of recognition for a life devoted to love and loyalty.

A Legacy That Lives On

Hachiko passed away on March 8, 1935, near Shibuya Station. His death marked the end of an era, but his legacy was just beginning. News of his passing spread far and wide, and people mourned him as a national hero.

Today, the statue of Hachiko stands as a beloved landmark at Shibuya Station, a meeting spot for countless people and a reminder of the enduring power of loyalty. Every year on March 8, a ceremony is held in his honor, attended by dog lovers from around the world.

Hachiko's story has inspired books, movies, and artworks, each retelling the tale of a dog whose love and loyalty knew no bounds. His unwavering devotion serves as a poignant reminder of the bonds we share with our animal companions—a bond rooted in trust, love, and the quiet promise of always being there for each other.

Lessons from Hachiko

Hachiko's story is more than just a heartwarming tale; it's a testament to the depth of the human-animal bond. In a world often marked by fleeting connections, his steadfast loyalty reminds us of the values that truly matter: love, patience, and faithfulness.

For those who visit Shibuya Station today, the statue of

Hachiko isn't just a piece of history; it's a symbol of the kind of loyalty we all aspire to have in our lives. It's a tribute to a humble Akita who showed the world what it means to love unconditionally—and to never stop waiting for the ones we hold dear.

***

Nine Years of Devotion: Hachiko's Daily Vigil at Shibuya Station After His Owner's Death

It's often said that dogs are creatures of habit, but Hachiko, a humble Akita from Japan, elevated this to an extraordinary level. His story of loyalty, displayed through his daily vigil at Shibuya Station, isn't just a tale of routine but one of undying devotion that continues to inspire people worldwide. For nine years, Hachiko waited—day in, day out—for his beloved master, Professor Hidesaburo Ueno, to return. Though his master was gone, Hachiko's heart never stopped believing.

The Day That Changed Everything

On a warm spring morning in May 1925, life unfolded as usual for Hachiko and Professor Ueno. The professor left for work at the University of Tokyo, with Hachiko accompanying him to Shibuya Station as he did every day. They shared a quiet moment of companionship before Ueno boarded the train, both unaware that this would be their final goodbye.

Tragically, Professor Ueno suffered a sudden brain hemorrhage while lecturing at the university and passed away. He never returned to the station that evening. Hachiko, unaware of the devastating news, waited patiently, scanning the faces of the passengers for the one he loved most.

A Routine That Became a Ritual

The following day, and every day after, Hachiko returned to Shibuya Station at precisely the same time his master's train would have arrived. Rain or shine, through the oppressive heat of summer and the biting cold of winter, Hachiko was there. He sat in the same spot, his expressive eyes full of hope and longing, a picture of quiet determination.

Initially, many commuters didn't notice the solitary dog sitting by the station gates. But as days turned into weeks and weeks into months, his presence became impossible to ignore. People began to talk, curious about why this loyal dog came to the station each day.

Hachiko's story soon spread through the local community. Vendors and station workers, moved by his persistence, started bringing him food and water. Children would stop to pet him, and passersby often paused to admire his resilience. Shibuya Station became more than just a transit hub; it became the setting for an extraordinary tale of love and loyalty.

A Symbol of Devotion

By the early 1930s, Hachiko's daily vigil had become the stuff of legend. A journalist's article in 1932 brought his story to national attention, dubbing him "Chuken Hachiko" or "Faithful Dog Hachiko." The article described the profound bond between Hachiko and Professor Ueno, capturing the hearts of readers across Japan.

People traveled from far and wide to see Hachiko. They marveled at his steadfastness and often left offerings at his station spot—a way of paying tribute to the little dog with the unshakable spirit. For many, Hachiko became a symbol of the kind of loyalty that people strive for but rarely achieve.

The Passing Years

As the years went by, Hachiko's once-pristine coat grew ragged, and his youthful energy waned. Yet his determination remained as strong as ever. Every evening, he made his way to the station, limping at times but always resolute. He never let age or hardship deter him from his mission.

Hachiko's presence was a comforting constant for the bustling crowds of Shibuya. In a rapidly changing world, his unwavering faith reminded people of the enduring power of love and devotion. Even those who had never met Professor Ueno felt the weight of Hachiko's story, as if they, too, were waiting for someone they had lost.

The Final Goodbye

On March 8, 1935, Hachiko's incredible journey came to an end. He was found lifeless on a street near Shibuya Station, his faithful heart having finally given out. News of his death spread quickly, and the entire nation mourned. Hachiko's passing marked the end of an era, but his story was far from over.

Hachiko's body was preserved and displayed at the National Museum of Nature and Science in Tokyo, where visitors continue to pay their respects. His ashes were buried beside Professor Ueno's grave, symbolically reuniting the two companions at last.

A Legacy That Lives On

Today, Hachiko's bronze statue stands proudly outside Shibuya Station, a timeless tribute to his loyalty. Travelers and locals alike gather at the statue, often meeting under its watchful gaze. March 8 has become an unofficial day of remembrance for Hachiko, with ceremonies held to honor his legacy.

Hachiko's story has been immortalized in books, movies, and countless retellings. But beyond the fame, it is the quiet simplicity of his devotion that continues to resonate. His tale is a reminder of the profound bond between humans and dogs, a bond built on trust, love, and an unwavering promise to always be there.

The Lessons of Hachiko

Hachiko's nine years of waiting teach us something rare and beautiful about loyalty. In a world that often feels hurried and transient, his story reminds us of the power of patience and faith. It challenges us to reflect on the relationships we hold dear and to ask ourselves if we, too, are capable of such devotion.

As you think about Hachiko sitting at Shibuya Station, day after day, you might wonder: What gave him the strength to keep waiting? The answer lies in the simplicity of his love. Hachiko didn't wait because he expected something in return. He waited because love made it impossible for him to do anything else.

Hachiko's story is more than a tale of a dog's loyalty; it's a testament to the kind of love that transcends time, distance, and even death. It's a love that, nine decades later, continues to inspire and uplift us—a love that truly knows no bounds.

UNWAVERING LOYALTY: DOGS WHO CHANGED LIVES

***

Legacy and Inspiration: How Hachiko's Story Continues to Inspire Loyalty Worldwide

The story of Hachiko is more than just a tale of one dog's devotion to his owner; it is a universal symbol of loyalty, love, and the unbreakable bonds that connect us to those we hold dear. Decades after his passing, Hachiko's legacy continues to inspire people across the globe. From statues and ceremonies to literature and film, his story has transcended borders and cultures, touching the hearts of countless admirers.

Hachiko's life may have been simple, but the impact of his unwavering loyalty is profound. It challenges us to reflect on our own relationships and what it means to truly stand by someone. Let's explore how Hachiko's story has been preserved and how his enduring legacy continues to inspire loyalty worldwide.

A Symbol of Devotion in Japan

In his homeland of Japan, Hachiko is more than a beloved dog—he is a cultural icon. His statue at Shibuya Station has become a landmark, a place where people gather not only to meet but also to honor his extraordinary devotion. It is one of the most photographed spots in Tokyo, and visitors from around the world make it a point to see the bronze Akita that stands as a testament to loyalty.

Every year on March 8, the anniversary of Hachiko's passing, a memorial ceremony is held at the statue. Dog lovers and admirers come together to celebrate his life, laying flowers and reflecting on the values he represents. These gatherings remind us that loyalty and love are universal virtues, transcending time and language.

Beyond Shibuya, Hachiko's influence extends to schools, where children learn about his story as part of their curriculum. Teachers use Hachiko's tale to instill values of kindness, patience, and loyalty. In this way, Hachiko's legacy lives on in the hearts of each new generation.

Inspiration Around the World

Hachiko's story has not been confined to Japan; it has inspired people worldwide. His tale has been adapted into books, movies, and even children's stories, each retelling capturing the essence of his loyalty.

One of the most notable adaptations is the 2009 Hollywood film *Hachi: A Dog's Tale*, starring Richard Gere. The movie reimagines Hachiko's story in an American setting, bringing his tale to an even broader audience. It was met with widespread acclaim, praised for its heartfelt depiction of Hachiko's devotion. The film continues to be a favorite among dog lovers, sparking emotional connections and introducing new fans to the legendary Akita.

Social media and online platforms have also played a role in spreading Hachiko's story. Memes, videos, and posts featuring Hachiko's legacy frequently go viral, serving as modern-day reminders of his timeless message. In a world that often feels fast-paced and disconnected, his story resonates as a beacon of steadfast love and commitment.

Lessons for Life and Relationships

Hachiko's story carries profound lessons that apply to all aspects of life. At its core, his unwavering loyalty challenges us to reflect on our own relationships and commitments.

1. **The Power of Patience**: Hachiko waited every day for nine years, demonstrating a level of patience that is rarely seen. In our own lives, his story encourages us to cultivate patience in our relationships, whether with loved ones, colleagues, or friends.
2. **Love Without Conditions**: Hachiko's devotion was pure and unconditional. He didn't wait because he hoped for a reward; he waited because his heart couldn't do otherwise. This selflessness reminds us of the beauty of giving love freely, without expecting anything in return.
3. **Faith in the Face of Loss**: Hachiko's persistence after the loss of his owner is a poignant example of resilience. It reminds us that even in moments of grief, love can provide a sense of purpose and strength.

Hachiko's Influence on Animal Welfare

Hachiko's story has also played a role in raising awareness about the emotional depth of animals and the bonds they share with humans. His tale has inspired countless people to adopt pets and treat them with the love and respect they deserve.

Organizations around the world have drawn upon Hachiko's legacy to promote animal welfare campaigns, emphasizing the importance of kindness to animals. His story serves as a reminder that dogs—and all animals—are capable of incredible emotional connections and should be treated as cherished members of our families.

In addition, Hachiko's breed, the Akita, gained recognition and admiration thanks to his story. Once relatively unknown outside Japan, the Akita is now celebrated for its loyalty and intelligence, with many owners citing Hachiko as their inspiration for choosing the breed.

A Legacy for the Ages

What makes Hachiko's story so enduring is its simplicity. It is not a tale of grand gestures or dramatic events but of quiet, steadfast love. This simplicity is what makes it so relatable and universally understood.

Hachiko reminds us that loyalty and love are not measured by words but by actions. His daily vigil at Shibuya Station speaks volumes about the power of consistency and the depth of the bonds we share with those we love.

Even today, as technology and modern life create new distractions, Hachiko's story serves as a grounding force. It encourages us to pause, reflect, and prioritize the relationships that matter most.

Conclusion: A Legacy That Lives On

Hachiko's legacy is far more than the story of one dog; it is a celebration of loyalty in its purest form. It reminds us of the incredible capacity for love that exists in every corner of the world, from a busy train station in Tokyo to the hearts of those who hear his story.

As we honor Hachiko's memory, we also honor the countless

dogs—and other pets—who demonstrate similar devotion every day. They remind us to cherish the connections that make life meaningful, to be loyal to those we care about, and to love with our whole hearts.

Hachiko may no longer sit at Shibuya Station, but his spirit remains there, inspiring millions who pass through its gates. His legacy is a timeless reminder that the bonds we share with our dogs—and each other—are what truly make life extraordinary.

UNWAVERING LOYALTY: DOGS WHO CHANGED LIVES

***

Capitan – The Cemetery Guardian

The Lost Master: Capitan's Incredible Journey to His Owner's Grave After His Passing

In a small Argentine town, a German Shepherd named Capitan captivated the hearts of many with a remarkable display of love and loyalty. Much like the legendary Hachiko, Capitan's story is one of devotion that transcends life and death. For years, this loyal dog made his home in a cemetery, guarding the grave of his beloved owner. His journey, filled with heartache and faithfulness, stands as a testament to the depth of the bond between humans and their canine companions.

The Bond Between a Boy and His Dog

Capitan was a spirited German Shepherd who belonged to Miguel Guzmán, a resident of Villa Carlos Paz in Argentina. Miguel had adopted Capitan as a gift for his young son, Damian. From the moment Capitan bounded into their lives, he became much more than a pet—he was a cherished member of the family.

Miguel and Capitan shared a special connection. They would often go on long walks together, Miguel talking to Capitan as if he were a close friend. Capitan, with his intelligent eyes and attentive demeanor, seemed to understand every word. Their bond was one of quiet companionship and mutual affection, the kind that only dogs and their humans can share.

But life, as it often does, took an unexpected turn. In March 2006, Miguel passed away suddenly. The family was devastated, and so was Capitan. He became restless and agitated, his behavior reflecting the deep loss he felt.

A Mysterious Journey to the Cemetery

Not long after Miguel's funeral, something extraordinary happened. Capitan disappeared. The Guzmán family searched high and low for their beloved dog but couldn't find him. Days turned into weeks, and the family began to fear the worst.

Then, one day, while visiting Miguel's grave, the family found Capitan lying by the headstone. His eyes, filled with quiet sorrow, told the story of his grief. What amazed everyone was that Capitan had never been taken to the cemetery before. How he found Miguel's grave remains a mystery.

Some speculate that Capitan followed Miguel's scent to the cemetery. Others believe that his deep bond with Miguel guided him there, a testament to the unexplainable connection between dogs and their humans. Regardless of how he found his way, what mattered was that Capitan had chosen to stay.

A Vigil That Lasted Years

From that day on, Capitan rarely left Miguel's grave. He would lie by the headstone during the day and patrol the cemetery grounds at night, almost as if he were guarding his master. Local cemetery workers began to take notice of the loyal dog, who seemed to understand the sanctity of his surroundings.

The workers, moved by Capitan's devotion, provided him with food and water. They recounted how, every evening as the sun set, Capitan would rest his head on Miguel's grave, as if seeking comfort from the man he loved so deeply.

Capitan's vigil lasted for over a decade. Despite efforts by the Guzmán family to bring him home, Capitan always returned to the cemetery. It was as if he had made a solemn promise to Miguel to stay by his side, even in death.

A Community United by Loyalty

Capitan's story quickly spread beyond Villa Carlos Paz, capturing the attention of people across Argentina and around the world. Journalists, animal lovers, and visitors came to the cemetery to see the loyal dog who refused to abandon his master.

For many, Capitan's devotion was a source of inspiration. His story reminded people of the enduring power of love and loyalty, qualities often overshadowed in the rush of daily life. It also sparked conversations about the emotional intelligence of dogs and the deep connections they share with humans.

The cemetery workers became Capitan's second family, ensuring he was cared for as he aged. His fur began to gray, and his steps slowed, but his resolve never wavered. Capitan's presence brought a sense of peace to the cemetery, his quiet vigil a reminder of the bonds that extend beyond life.

The Final Goodbye

In February 2018, after 12 years of faithfully guarding Miguel's grave, Capitan passed away. His death was met with an outpouring of grief from the local community and beyond. For many, it felt as though they were saying goodbye to a hero, a dog who had demonstrated the kind of love and loyalty that humans often strive to emulate.

Capitan was laid to rest near Miguel's grave, ensuring that, even in death, they would not be separated. The cemetery workers, who had cared for Capitan as one of their own, marked his resting place with a simple tribute. It wasn't grand or elaborate, but it was deeply heartfelt—a reflection of the humble yet profound legacy Capitan left behind.

Lessons from Capitan's Story

Capitan's incredible journey to Miguel's grave and his unwavering loyalty teach us profound lessons about love, loss, and the strength of bonds that defy explanation.

1. **The Power of Connection**: Capitan's ability to find Miguel's grave, despite never having been shown its location, speaks to the depth of their connection. It's a reminder that love can transcend physical boundaries and logic.
2. **Loyalty in Action**: Capitan's refusal to leave Miguel's side, even after death, exemplifies the purest form of loyalty.

His story challenges us to reflect on our own commitments and how we show up for the people we care about.
3. **Healing Through Devotion**: While Capitan's vigil was born of grief, it also brought comfort—to himself, to the Guzmán family, and to the countless people who heard his story. His loyalty became a source of healing and inspiration for all who knew him.

A Legacy of Love

Capitan's story continues to be celebrated as a testament to the extraordinary bond between humans and dogs. He showed the world that love isn't confined to life; it's something that endures, even when separated by death.

Today, visitors to Villa Carlos Paz still speak of Capitan with admiration and affection. His legacy lives on in the hearts of those who were touched by his story, a reminder that loyalty is one of the greatest gifts we can offer.

As we reflect on Capitan's incredible journey, we are reminded of the simple yet profound truth that dogs teach us every day: Love, when given freely and unconditionally, has the power to transcend all boundaries. And for that, Capitan will always be remembered—not just as a loyal dog, but as a symbol of devotion that knows no bounds.

UNWAVERING LOYALTY: DOGS WHO CHANGED LIVES

***

Years of Vigilance: Capitan's Commitment to Sleeping by the Grave for Over a Decade

In a world often consumed by fleeting relationships and distractions, the story of Capitan, a devoted German Shepherd, serves as a heartwarming reminder of the enduring power of loyalty. For over a decade, Capitan stood as a sentinel of love, refusing to leave the side of his late owner, Miguel Guzmán. His unwavering commitment, marked by his daily and nightly presence at Miguel's grave, turned a small cemetery in Villa Carlos Paz, Argentina, into a symbol of the extraordinary bond between a man and his dog.

A Devastating Loss and a Lonely Heart

Capitan's life changed forever in March 2006 when his owner, Miguel, passed away unexpectedly. Miguel and Capitan shared a special relationship—one built on love, trust, and companionship. Capitan had been a gift from Miguel to his young son, Damian, but it was clear from the start that the German Shepherd and Miguel shared a unique connection.

Miguel's death left a void not only in the lives of his family but also in Capitan's heart. Dogs, with their keen emotional sensitivity, often grieve in ways that mirror human loss. Capitan began to exhibit signs of restlessness, wandering the streets and searching for something—or someone—missing from his life.

A Journey Guided by Love

One day, not long after Miguel's funeral, Capitan vanished from the Guzmán family's home. The family searched tirelessly for their beloved dog but found no trace of him. Weeks later, they made a startling discovery. On a visit to the local cemetery, where Miguel was buried, they found Capitan lying on his owner's grave, his body curled protectively around the headstone.

The family was both amazed and deeply moved. Capitan had never been taken to the cemetery and had no way of knowing where Miguel was buried. How he found his way there remains a mystery. Some attribute his journey to an extraordinary sense of smell, while others believe it was guided by the invisible thread of love connecting him to his master.

An Unbreakable Routine

From that day forward, the cemetery became Capitan's home. Every evening as the sun dipped below the horizon, Capitan would curl up by Miguel's grave, settling into a quiet vigil that lasted through the night. During the day, he would roam the cemetery grounds, sometimes greeting visitors or napping in the shade of a tree, but he always returned to Miguel's side.

The cemetery workers, touched by Capitan's devotion, began to care for him. They provided food, water, and a safe place to rest during bad weather. Yet, despite their kindness, Capitan's loyalty never wavered—his true home was by Miguel's grave.

Over the years, Capitan's routine became a symbol of steadfast love. His nightly vigil was not just a habit but a heartfelt expression of his enduring bond with Miguel. Through scorching summers, bitter winters, and relentless rain, Capitan's commitment remained unshaken.

A Story That Captured the World

Word of Capitan's extraordinary loyalty spread beyond Villa Carlos Paz, capturing the attention of people across Argentina and eventually the world. Local newspapers first reported the story, and soon it was picked up by international outlets. Readers were moved by the tale of the German Shepherd who refused to abandon his owner, even in death.

Capitan's story struck a universal chord. It resonated with anyone who had ever experienced love, loss, or the longing to hold onto someone dear. For many, Capitan became a symbol of the kind of loyalty that is often elusive in human relationships.

Visitors began flocking to the cemetery, not just to pay their respects to Miguel but also to see Capitan. They brought treats, toys, and blankets for the loyal dog, many leaving with tears in their eyes after witnessing his quiet vigil. Capitan's story reminded people of the pure, unconditional love that dogs so often give without expecting anything in return.

The Challenges of Vigilance

As the years passed, Capitan grew older. His once-strong body began to show signs of wear, his gait slowing and his fur graying. Yet his spirit remained as resolute as ever.

Life at the cemetery was not without its challenges. Capitan faced harsh weather conditions, occasional illnesses, and the loneliness of a life spent away from his human family. Despite these hardships, he stayed true to his purpose. The cemetery workers did their best to care for him, even taking him to the vet when needed. They became his second family, but Capitan's heart remained firmly tethered to Miguel.

The Guzmán family, too, visited Capitan at the cemetery, often trying to coax him to come home with them. But each time, Capitan returned to Miguel's grave, as if bound by an invisible promise. His loyalty was so profound that it left even seasoned animal behaviorists in awe.

The End of an Era

In February 2018, Capitan's incredible journey came to an end. After 12 years of unwavering vigilance, he passed away near Miguel's grave, his faithful heart finally at rest. The cemetery workers who had cared for him buried him near his beloved owner, ensuring that they would remain together in death as they had been in life.

News of Capitan's passing was met with an outpouring of grief and tributes from around the world. For those who had followed his story, it felt like the loss of a personal friend—a dog who had embodied the values of love, loyalty, and resilience in a way few humans ever could.

Lessons from Capitan's Vigil

Capitan's commitment to Miguel's grave offers profound lessons for all of us.

1. **Loyalty Beyond Circumstance**: Capitan's dedication was not tied to convenience or reward. It was a pure and unwavering devotion that challenges us to consider how

we show loyalty in our own lives.
2. **The Healing Power of Love**: While Capitan's vigil was born of grief, it also brought comfort—to himself, to Miguel's family, and to everyone who heard his story. His loyalty became a source of healing and inspiration.
3. **The Strength of Simple Acts**: Capitan's daily routine was simple, yet its impact was extraordinary. It reminds us that even the smallest acts of love and commitment can leave an indelible mark.

A Legacy That Lives On

Today, Capitan's story continues to be celebrated as a timeless example of the bond between humans and dogs. His life reminds us that loyalty and love can endure beyond life itself, transcending the barriers of time and space.

Capitan's grave, marked with love and respect, serves as a quiet tribute to a dog who taught the world what it means to stay true. His story inspires us to cherish the connections that matter most, to honor our commitments, and to love without reservation.

As we reflect on Capitan's remarkable vigil, we are reminded that loyalty isn't just a virtue—it's a legacy. Capitan's unwavering presence by Miguel's side was more than an act of love; it was a promise kept. And in that promise, we find the heart of his extraordinary story—a story that will continue to inspire for generations to come.

UNWAVERING LOYALTY: DOGS WHO CHANGED LIVES

***

A Community's Love: How the Locals Supported and Celebrated Capitan's Loyalty

In the quiet town of Villa Carlos Paz, Argentina, a German Shepherd named Capitan captured the hearts of an entire community. His story of unwavering loyalty to his late owner, Miguel Guzmán, resonated not only with the Guzmán family but with the locals who witnessed his incredible devotion firsthand. For over a decade, Capitan made the cemetery his home, standing guard over Miguel's grave. In return, the community embraced Capitan, offering care, support, and recognition that turned his life into a living testament of love and loyalty.

An Unlikely Guardian at the Cemetery

When Capitan first appeared at the cemetery, locals were astonished. They couldn't understand how the dog had found his way to Miguel's grave, as he had never been shown its location. Some speculated it was his keen sense of smell, while others believed it was a deeper, almost spiritual connection that led him there.

Initially, cemetery workers thought Capitan might be a stray. But they quickly realized he wasn't just another wandering dog—he had a purpose. Capitan spent his days and nights at the same grave, his eyes filled with a quiet sorrow that moved everyone who saw him.

The cemetery workers were the first to take Capitan under their wing. Recognizing his loyalty, they provided him with food, water, and a sheltered spot to rest during inclement weather. They admired his steadfastness, noting how he never strayed far from the grave, even when other dogs came by or visitors tried to distract him.

A Town Rallies Behind Capitan

As news of Capitan's story spread, the people of Villa Carlos Paz began to take notice. Locals started visiting the cemetery, not just to pay their respects to their loved ones but to see Capitan. He became something of a local legend, a symbol of loyalty and love that brought people together.

Families brought blankets and treats to keep him comfortable. Children, wide-eyed with wonder, would sit quietly near him, as if hoping to absorb some of his steadfast devotion. Tourists passing through the town often stopped by the cemetery after hearing about the dog who wouldn't leave his master's side.

Capitan's presence created a unique sense of unity in the community. He wasn't just Miguel's dog anymore—he belonged to everyone. The townspeople adopted him in spirit, ensuring he had everything he needed to continue his vigil. For many, caring for Capitan became a way of honoring the values he represented: love, loyalty, and the power of a bond that transcends death.

The Role of the Cemetery Workers

The cemetery workers played a pivotal role in Capitan's story. They were the first to recognize the significance of his vigil and took it upon themselves to ensure his well-being. Over the years, they formed a deep bond with Capitan, treating him like a colleague and a friend.

These workers often shared anecdotes about Capitan with visitors, describing how he would roam the cemetery grounds during the day but always return to Miguel's grave by evening. They marveled at his intelligence and gentle demeanor, noting how he seemed to understand the sanctity of the place.

When Capitan grew older and began to show signs of aging, the cemetery workers took him to the vet for check-ups. They were deeply invested in his health, knowing that his continued presence brought comfort and inspiration to countless people.

A Beacon of Hope and Inspiration

Capitan's story wasn't just about loyalty; it was also about the healing power of love. Many people who visited the cemetery found solace in watching him. His quiet vigil reminded them of the enduring connections we share with those we've lost.

One visitor, grieving the recent loss of a family member, said, "Seeing Capitan here makes me believe that love doesn't end with death. It carries on, just like he carries on for Miguel."

Capitan became a source of comfort for those mourning their loved ones. His presence was a reminder that grief, while painful, could also be a testament to the depth of love shared.

Celebrating Capitan's Legacy

As Capitan's fame grew, so did the efforts to celebrate his incredible story. Local media outlets ran features on him, sharing his tale with a broader audience. Journalists and animal lovers from across the country visited Villa Carlos Paz to meet the loyal dog who had touched so many lives.

The community organized events to honor Capitan, raising

awareness about the special bond between humans and dogs. Schools incorporated his story into lessons about love and loyalty, teaching children the importance of these values. For many, Capitan became a symbol of what it means to stay true to those we care about, even in the face of loss.

When Capitan passed away in 2018, the town mourned as if they had lost a dear friend. The cemetery workers, who had cared for him for over a decade, buried him near Miguel's grave, ensuring that the bond between them would remain unbroken.

The Ripple Effect of Capitan's Story

Capitan's loyalty didn't just impact those in Villa Carlos Paz; it inspired people around the world. His story was shared in newspapers, blogs, and social media posts, touching hearts far beyond the small Argentine town.

Animal welfare organizations used Capitan's tale to highlight the emotional depth of dogs and their capacity for love. Some even launched campaigns encouraging pet adoption, urging people to find their own Capitan among the countless animals in need of homes.

For the locals, Capitan's impact was deeply personal. He reminded them of the importance of community, kindness, and the simple yet profound act of showing up for those who matter.

A Love That Endures

The story of Capitan is, at its core, a story about love—the kind of love that doesn't waver, even in the face of loss. It's about the connections that tie us to one another, the quiet acts of care that bind a community, and the ways we find meaning in honoring those we've lost.

Capitan's vigil at Miguel's grave became more than just a testament to loyalty; it became a source of inspiration for an entire town and beyond. His unwavering presence brought people together, reminding them of the values that truly matter.

Today, Capitan's legacy lives on, not just in the memories of those who knew him but in the countless lives he touched. His story continues to inspire acts of kindness, loyalty, and love, proving that even in the simplest acts, there is extraordinary power.

Capitan wasn't just a dog—he was a symbol of devotion, a bridge between grief and healing, and a reminder that love, when given freely and unconditionally, can change the world.

UNWAVERING LOYALTY: DOGS WHO CHANGED LIVES

***

Bobbie – The Wonder Dog

The Long Journey Home: Bobbie's 2,500-Mile Trek Across the U.S. to Reunite with His Family

In the annals of extraordinary animal tales, few stories capture the imagination and the heart quite like that of Bobbie the Wonder Dog. A humble collie-mix from Silverton, Oregon, Bobbie became a national sensation in the 1920s when he accomplished what seemed impossible: a 2,500-mile journey across the United States to find his way back to his family. His odyssey, filled with danger, determination, and the sheer power of love, serves as a testament to the unbreakable bond between humans and their canine companions.

A Beloved Member of the Brazier Family

Bobbie was more than just a pet to the Brazier family; he was a cherished member of their household. Owned by Frank and Elizabeth Brazier, Bobbie was a collie-English shepherd mix known for his gentle nature and boundless affection. He was particularly close to the Braziers' two daughters, who adored his playful demeanor and unwavering loyalty.

In the summer of 1923, the Braziers embarked on a road trip from their home in Silverton to Wolcott, Indiana, to visit relatives. It was a long journey, but they brought Bobbie along, confident he would enjoy the adventure as much as they did.

Tragedy struck during a stop in Indiana. Bobbie became separated from his family in a busy town. Despite frantic efforts to find him, he was nowhere to be seen. The Braziers were heartbroken. After several days of searching and posting notices, they had no choice but to continue their trip and return home, devastated at leaving Bobbie behind.

The Beginning of an Epic Journey

What the Braziers didn't know was that Bobbie had no intention of staying behind. Somehow, this determined dog resolved to find his way back to them, despite the incredible distance and the countless challenges ahead.

Bobbie's journey began in an unfamiliar landscape filled with obstacles. He faced harsh weather conditions, from blistering summer heat to freezing winter temperatures. He traversed rivers, deserts, forests, and mountain ranges, encountering wild animals and navigating through towns and cities.

His journey wasn't without help. Along the way, kind-hearted strangers took notice of the thin, weary dog. Many offered food, shelter, and care, noting his determination to keep moving westward. These acts of kindness became vital to Bobbie's survival. Despite his exhaustion and injuries, including worn-down paws from endless walking, Bobbie pressed on, guided by an unshakable instinct to reunite with his family.

The Homecoming That Stunned the World

Six months after his disappearance, Bobbie's remarkable journey came to an end. In February 1924, he appeared in Silverton, astonishing everyone who saw him. He was thin, his fur matted and ragged, and his body showed signs of the grueling trek—but he was alive.

When Bobbie reached the Brazier family's home, the reunion was nothing short of miraculous. The family was overwhelmed with emotion, barely able to believe their eyes. Bobbie's excitement was equally palpable as he greeted each member of his beloved family. Despite the long months of separation and the countless miles he had traveled, his joy at being home was undeniable.

The story quickly spread, captivating the nation. People marveled at Bobbie's extraordinary ability to navigate an impossible distance and survive the perils of the journey. Scientists, animal behaviorists, and ordinary citizens alike were fascinated by the mystery of how he managed to find his way back.

A Hero in the Spotlight

Bobbie's incredible journey turned him into a national celebrity. Newspapers across the country published his story, dubbing him "Bobbie the Wonder Dog." He received letters, gifts, and even offers of sponsorship from admirers who were inspired by his loyalty and resilience.

In the months following his return, the Braziers were inundated with visitors who wanted to meet the legendary dog. Bobbie became the subject of countless anecdotes, with people along his route coming forward to share their own encounters with him. Their accounts confirmed the unbelievable distance he had traveled and painted a picture of a dog who never gave up, even in the face of overwhelming odds.

Bobbie's fame reached its peak when he was invited to appear at the Portland Home Show in 1924. There, he was presented with a jewel-studded harness and collar as a tribute to his incredible achievement. Crowds gathered to see him, and he was treated like a true hero.

Lessons from Bobbie's Journey

Bobbie's story resonates because it speaks to the universal values of love, loyalty, and perseverance. His journey wasn't just a feat of physical endurance; it was an emotional odyssey that reminded people of the depth of the bond between humans and animals.

1. **Love Knows No Bounds**: Bobbie's unwavering determination to find his family demonstrates the power of love to overcome even the most insurmountable challenges.
2. **The Kindness of Strangers**: Bobbie's survival depended on the compassion of people who helped him along the way. His story highlights the importance of acts of kindness and the impact they can have on someone—or some dog—in need.
3. **Never Give Up**: Bobbie's perseverance in the face of adversity is a lesson for all of us. His journey serves as a reminder that even when the odds seem impossible, determination can lead us to where we're meant to be.

A Legacy That Lives On

Bobbie's story didn't end with his triumphant return. He lived out the rest of his days as a beloved member of the Brazier family, enjoying the comforts of home that he had fought so hard to reclaim. He passed away in 1927, but his legacy continues to inspire.

In his honor, the town of Silverton erected a statue and mural commemorating his incredible journey. Every year, the town celebrates Bobbie's story with events that bring the community together, reminding them of the power of loyalty and the enduring bond between humans and their canine companions.

Bobbie's tale has been passed down through generations, capturing the hearts of dog lovers and adventurers alike. His journey is more than a story of a dog finding his way home; it's a testament to the strength of the connections that tie us to those we love, no matter how far apart we may be.

Even today, nearly a century later, Bobbie's story continues to inspire awe and admiration. It reminds us of the extraordinary potential within all living beings and the profound impact of love and loyalty in our lives. Bobbie wasn't just a dog—he was a symbol of hope, determination, and the enduring power of home.

UNWAVERING LOYALTY: DOGS WHO CHANGED LIVES

***

Facing Unthinkable Odds: How Bobbie Overcame Harsh Weather and Dangerous Terrain

When Bobbie the Wonder Dog embarked on his 2,500-mile journey to reunite with his family in Silverton, Oregon, he faced challenges that would test even the most seasoned adventurers. Crossing rivers, trudging through snow, and navigating deserts were just some of the trials that lay ahead. Yet, through it all, Bobbie demonstrated resilience and determination that defied the odds. His odyssey was a testament not only to his physical endurance but to the strength of his love and loyalty.

Through the Scorching Heat

Bobbie began his trek during the late summer months, making his way westward from Indiana. The Midwest in August is known for its blistering heat, with temperatures often soaring above 90°F. For a dog traveling on foot, with no clear access to consistent water or shade, the conditions were brutal.

Locals along his route recounted stories of a thin, dusty dog arriving in small towns and seeking shelter from the sun. Some recalled how he would rest under trees or near streams before continuing his journey. His paws, worn from walking on hot pavement and dirt roads, bore the marks of his determination.

One farmer in Illinois remembered seeing Bobbie collapse near a well on his property. The farmer offered him water and food, marveling at the dog's resolve. Despite his obvious exhaustion, Bobbie stayed only long enough to regain his strength before setting off again. His focus never wavered, even under the punishing sun.

Battling the Bitter Cold

As summer gave way to fall and then winter, Bobbie encountered an entirely new set of challenges. The biting cold of the Great Plains and the Rocky Mountains presented a stark contrast to the sweltering heat he had faced earlier. Snow-covered landscapes stretched endlessly before him, making navigation even more difficult.

Bobbie's coat, while thick, wasn't enough to completely shield him from freezing temperatures. He had to rely on his instincts to find warmth, often seeking refuge in barns, sheds, or under porches. People who encountered him during this time noted his persistence, even as the weather grew increasingly unforgiving.

One family in Colorado recalled how Bobbie appeared on their doorstep during a blizzard. The family took him in for the night, providing him with warmth, food, and rest. Despite their kindness, Bobbie didn't linger. By morning, he was back on the road, braving the icy winds and deep snowdrifts.

Crossing the Rockies was perhaps the most perilous part of Bobbie's journey. The treacherous mountain terrain posed a significant risk, with steep cliffs, hidden ice patches, and scarce food sources. Yet Bobbie pressed on, driven by an instinctive pull toward his home.

Navigating the Deserts and Forests

Between the mountains and his final destination lay the arid expanses of the American West. Crossing the deserts of Utah and eastern Oregon would have been daunting for any traveler, human or canine. The barren landscapes offered little in the way of sustenance or shelter, and the extreme temperature swings—from scorching days to freezing nights—added to the difficulty.

Bobbie's resourcefulness became his greatest asset. He learned to drink from small puddles and forage for scraps wherever he could find them. His keen senses helped him avoid many of the dangers lurking in the desert, such as rattlesnakes and scorpions.

In the forests of western Oregon, Bobbie faced a different kind of challenge. Dense underbrush, thick canopies, and unpredictable wildlife made the final stretch of his journey arduous. Bobbie had to navigate through towering pines and tangled vegetation, relying on his instincts to stay on the right path.

One lumberjack recalled seeing Bobbie limping through the woods near the Cascade foothills. The man offered him food and marveled at his persistence. Despite his injuries and the toll the journey had taken on his body, Bobbie's resolve never faltered.

Surviving on Kindness

Throughout his journey, Bobbie encountered countless strangers who became part of his incredible story. Their acts of kindness—providing food, water, shelter, and care—were instrumental in helping him overcome the challenges he faced.

In Kansas, a store owner shared how Bobbie had wandered into town and approached him with a cautious but hopeful demeanor. Touched by the dog's determination, the man gave him a meal and a warm place to rest for the night.

In Utah, a group of railroad workers noticed Bobbie following the tracks. They bandaged his injured paws and fed him scraps from their lunchboxes. The workers were in awe of the dog's apparent sense of purpose, describing him as "a traveler on a mission."

These interactions not only sustained Bobbie physically but also revealed the deep connection between humans and animals. People who helped Bobbie often remarked on the clarity of his purpose and the strength of his spirit.

The Power of Resilience

Bobbie's journey was more than a physical feat; it was a testament to his extraordinary resilience. Each challenge he faced—the searing heat, the freezing cold, the rugged terrain—could have easily defeated him. Yet, he pushed forward, driven by an unshakable bond with his family.

This resilience was rooted in his unwavering loyalty. For Bobbie, the journey wasn't just about survival; it was about love. His determination to reunite with his family transcended the obstacles in his path, inspiring everyone who heard his story.

Even as his body endured hardship, Bobbie's spirit remained unbroken. His ability to adapt, persevere, and trust in the kindness of strangers spoke volumes about the depth of his character.

A Legacy of Courage and Love

Bobbie's incredible journey is a powerful reminder of the strength and resilience that love can inspire. His story continues to captivate hearts, not just because of the challenges he overcame but because of the unwavering devotion that fueled his odyssey.

For those who followed Bobbie's tale, his perseverance in the face of unthinkable odds became a symbol of hope and determination. His journey reminds us that no obstacle is insurmountable when love is the driving force.

Even today, nearly a century later, Bobbie's story serves as an inspiration. It's a testament to the enduring bond between humans and their canine companions, and to the extraordinary lengths that loyalty and love can take us—even across thousands of miles of treacherous terrain.

***

Recognition and Celebration: Bobbie's Fame and Lasting Legacy in Oregon

Bobbie the Wonder Dog's incredible 2,500-mile journey back to his family didn't just inspire awe and admiration—it cemented his place in Oregon's history and in the hearts of people around the world. His story of loyalty and determination resonated deeply with those who heard it, making him a celebrated figure whose legacy continues to be honored nearly a century later.

From national headlines to heartfelt community tributes, Bobbie's fame grew rapidly after his miraculous return to Silverton. He wasn't just a dog who found his way home; he became a symbol of unwavering love and resilience. His journey sparked celebrations, inspired art and literature, and left an indelible mark on his hometown and beyond.

A Hero's Welcome in Silverton

When Bobbie limped into Silverton in February 1924, his family was overwhelmed with joy and disbelief. News of his incredible journey quickly spread through the small town, and it wasn't long before the entire community came together to celebrate their local hero.

Silverton embraced Bobbie as more than just a dog; he became a symbol of hope and perseverance. The town held parades in his honor, with residents lining the streets to catch a glimpse of the Wonder Dog who had defied all odds to return home.

Children in Silverton told his story at school, while adults recounted the tale at social gatherings. Bobbie's return became a point of pride for the town, and he was treated as a beloved celebrity.

National and International Fame

Bobbie's story didn't stay confined to Silverton. Newspapers across the country picked up the tale, dubbing him "Bobbie the Wonder Dog." His remarkable journey captivated a nation eager for stories of inspiration and resilience.

He received countless letters from admirers, many of whom shared their own experiences of loyalty and love with their pets. Some sent gifts, including collars, blankets, and treats, as tokens of appreciation for his incredible spirit.

Bobbie's fame reached a new height when he was invited to the Portland Home Show in 1924. Thousands of people attended the event to meet him, and he was presented with a jewel-studded harness and collar as a tribute to his extraordinary achievement. Bobbie's gentle demeanor and calm presence endeared him to everyone he met, and his popularity only grew.

Even internationally, Bobbie's story resonated with dog lovers and adventurers. Articles about his journey were published in Europe and beyond, spreading the message of his unwavering loyalty to audiences across the globe.

Honoring His Legacy in Art and Media

Bobbie's incredible journey inspired countless artists and writers. Poems, short stories, and even songs were written in his honor, capturing the essence of his remarkable journey.

One of the most enduring tributes to Bobbie is a mural in

downtown Silverton that depicts his journey and homecoming. Painted in vibrant colors, the mural stands as a testament to the town's love for their Wonder Dog and serves as a reminder of the incredible bond between humans and their canine companions.

In addition to the mural, a statue of Bobbie was erected near his final resting place. The statue portrays him in a proud, alert stance, symbolizing his resilience and determination. Visitors from all over the world come to pay their respects, leaving flowers, notes, and even dog treats at the base of the monument.

Bobbie's story has also been featured in books, documentaries, and children's stories, ensuring that his legacy continues to inspire new generations. His tale is often included in discussions of loyalty and perseverance, both in academic and cultural contexts.

A Community's Celebration of Loyalty

Silverton has made it a point to keep Bobbie's legacy alive. Each year, the town holds events to celebrate his story, bringing the community together in remembrance of their four-legged hero.

These events often include parades, storytelling sessions, and fundraisers for local animal shelters. Children dress up as Bobbie for costume contests, and residents share their own stories of beloved pets who have shown extraordinary loyalty.

The annual celebrations serve not only to honor Bobbie but also to promote the values his story represents: love, loyalty, and perseverance. They remind the community of the profound impact that animals can have on our lives and the importance of treating them with kindness and respect.

A Symbol of Hope and Love

Bobbie's story endures because it speaks to universal truths that resonate with people from all walks of life. His journey wasn't just a physical feat; it was a testament to the power of love and the unbreakable bond between humans and their pets.

In a world often filled with challenges and uncertainties, Bobbie's story offers hope. It reminds us that even in the face of overwhelming odds, resilience and loyalty can lead to extraordinary outcomes.

For the people of Silverton, Bobbie is more than a historical figure—he is a source of pride and inspiration. His tale is a reminder that greatness often comes in the form of quiet determination and an open heart.

Lessons from Bobbie's Legacy

Bobbie's incredible journey and the recognition he received afterward leave us with several lasting lessons:

- **The Power of Loyalty**: Bobbie's determination to return to his family shows us the depth of loyalty and love that animals are capable of. It challenges us to reflect on our own relationships and the lengths we would go for those we care about.
- **The Importance of Kindness**: Bobbie's survival depended on the kindness of strangers who helped him along the way. His story highlights the impact of small acts of compassion and the difference they can make in someone's—or some dog's—life.
- **Celebrating Connection**: Bobbie's legacy is a testament

to the enduring bond between humans and animals. His story reminds us of the joy and meaning that pets bring to our lives and the importance of honoring that connection.

A Legacy That Lives On

Nearly a century after his remarkable journey, Bobbie the Wonder Dog continues to inspire. His story is passed down through generations, shared in classrooms, and celebrated in his hometown of Silverton.

For those who visit the town or learn about Bobbie's tale, his legacy serves as a powerful reminder of the extraordinary potential within all living beings. His fame may have been born out of an incredible journey, but it endures because of the universal truths it represents: love, loyalty, and the unbreakable bond between a dog and his family.

Bobbie wasn't just a wonder dog; he was a symbol of hope, perseverance, and the profound connection that ties us to those we love. His story, like his spirit, will live on forever.

BOBBIE – THE WONDER DOG

***

Greyfriars Bobby – The Skye Terrier Who Stayed

A Master's Love and Loss: How Greyfriars Bobby's Owner's Death Defined His Life

The story of Greyfriars Bobby is one that touches the deepest corners of the heart, illustrating the profound bond between a dog and his master. Bobby, a small Skye Terrier, became a symbol of unwavering loyalty after the passing of his beloved owner, John Gray. Despite his diminutive size, Bobby's devotion to his master was immense, and his actions after John's death turned him into a legend that continues to inspire people around the world.

This chapter delves into the life of Greyfriars Bobby, exploring his early years with John Gray, the heartbreak of loss, and the enduring loyalty that defined his legacy. It is a story that reminds us of the extraordinary capacity of dogs to love unconditionally and to remain faithful, even in the face of sorrow and solitude.

A Simple Life of Companionship

Bobby's story begins in the bustling streets of 19th-century Edinburgh, Scotland. As a young Skye Terrier, Bobby found his place at the side of John Gray, a night watchman who walked the city's cobbled streets to ensure its safety. John, known for his gentle demeanor, quickly bonded with Bobby, and the two became inseparable.

For Bobby, life with John was simple yet fulfilling. They spent their days and nights together, with Bobby accompanying John on his nightly patrols. The little terrier would trot alongside his master, braving the cold Scottish nights, his small frame exuding energy and loyalty.

John's affection for Bobby was evident in the way he cared for him. Though John's job didn't afford him great wealth, he made sure Bobby was always fed, groomed, and loved. The two were a familiar sight in Edinburgh, their bond a testament to the enduring friendship between humans and their dogs.

The Heartbreak of Loss

In 1858, tragedy struck when John Gray fell ill with tuberculosis. Despite his strength and resilience, the disease took its toll, and John passed away. For Bobby, the loss was devastating. The man who had been his constant companion, protector, and friend was gone, leaving a void that the little dog could neither understand nor fill.

John was buried in Greyfriars Kirkyard, a historic cemetery in Edinburgh. While his passing marked the end of his earthly life, it was the beginning of Bobby's extraordinary vigil—a display of loyalty that would captivate the world.

For Bobby, the connection to John didn't end with his death. The bond they shared was more than physical; it was a deep emotional tie that transcended life and death. Bobby's response to John's passing was a poignant reminder of the depth of love that dogs are capable of.

A Lifetime of Vigilance

After John's burial, Bobby began a routine that would define the rest of his life. Every day, the little Skye Terrier made his way to Greyfriars Kirkyard, where he would sit by his master's grave. Rain or shine, summer or winter, Bobby's devotion never wavered.

The sight of the small dog keeping vigil at the gravesite quickly drew the attention of locals. At first, cemetery caretakers tried to shoo him away, but Bobby always found his way back. Over time, the townsfolk grew to admire his loyalty and began looking after him.

Despite the challenges of living outdoors, Bobby thrived under the care of the community. Locals brought him food and water, and some even built a small shelter to protect him from the elements. Bobby became a beloved figure in Edinburgh, a symbol of love and devotion that resonated deeply with everyone who encountered him.

The Community's Role in Bobby's Story

Bobby's presence at the cemetery not only honored John Gray's memory but also brought the community together. People from all walks of life, inspired by Bobby's loyalty, took it upon themselves to ensure his well-being.

One notable figure was a restaurant owner named James Brown, who fed Bobby regularly. Brown's generosity ensured that the little dog never went hungry, even during the harshest winters. The Edinburgh City Council also played a role in Bobby's care by providing him with a collar and officially recognizing him as the "watchdog" of Greyfriars Kirkyard.

Bobby's story reached beyond Edinburgh, captivating the hearts of people far and wide. Visitors from other cities, and eventually other countries, came to see the little dog whose loyalty had become legendary. For many, Bobby was a reminder of the power of love and the enduring bond between humans and their pets.

The End of a Remarkable Life

Bobby's vigil lasted for an incredible 14 years. In 1872, the little dog passed away, still faithful to the memory of his master. He was buried near John Gray's grave in Greyfriars Kirkyard, ensuring that the two companions would remain together in death as they had been in life.

Bobby's death marked the end of an era, but his story was far from over. His legacy lived on, not only in the hearts of those who knew him but also in the countless tales and tributes that would follow.

A Lasting Legacy

Today, Greyfriars Bobby's story continues to inspire people around the world. A statue of Bobby, erected in 1873 near the entrance to Greyfriars Kirkyard, stands as a tribute to his loyalty and devotion. The statue, with its lifelike depiction of the small Skye Terrier, is a beloved landmark in Edinburgh, attracting visitors who come to pay their respects and learn about his remarkable life.

Bobby's story has been immortalized in books, films, and folklore, ensuring that his legacy will never fade. He is a reminder of the incredible capacity for love that dogs possess and the profound impact they can have on our lives.

Lessons from Bobby's Loyalty

Greyfriars Bobby's story is more than just a tale of a loyal dog; it's a testament to the unbreakable bond between humans and animals. His actions after John Gray's death offer several important lessons:

- **The Depth of Devotion**: Bobby's unwavering loyalty to his master shows us the true meaning of love and commitment. His vigil is a powerful reminder of the strength of the bond between dogs and their owners.
- **The Power of Community**: The way the people of Edinburgh cared for Bobby highlights the importance of compassion and kindness. Their support ensured that Bobby's story could unfold as it did.
- **The Enduring Nature of Love**: Even after death, Bobby's love for John Gray remained steadfast. His story reminds us that love transcends time and space, leaving an enduring legacy that touches all who hear it.

Greyfriars Bobby's life was defined by his love for John Gray, a bond so strong that it outlasted his master's death and inspired generations to come. In his loyalty, we see a reflection of the best qualities of dogs: their unwavering love, their resilience, and their capacity to bring out the best in humanity.

Bobby wasn't just a dog; he was a symbol of the profound connection that exists between humans and their animal companions—a connection that, once formed, can never truly be broken.

UNWAVERING LOYALTY: DOGS WHO CHANGED LIVES

***

14 Years of Loyalty: Greyfriars Bobby's Daily Vigil at Greyfriars Kirkyard

When you wander through the historic streets of Edinburgh, it's hard to miss the stories woven into its cobbled paths and timeless architecture. Among these tales is one of unparalleled devotion—Greyfriars Bobby, a small Skye Terrier whose loyalty to his owner transcended life itself. Bobby spent 14 years keeping watch at his master's grave in Greyfriars Kirkyard, capturing the hearts of locals and visitors alike. His vigil stands as one of history's most moving examples of love and loyalty.

This chapter delves into the extraordinary commitment of Greyfriars Bobby, recounting his unwavering devotion to his master, John Gray, and the community that rallied around him. Bobby's story reminds us of the profound bond between humans and their canine companions, a bond that endures even in the face of loss.

A Life Marked by Love

Before tragedy struck, Bobby's life was one of companionship and purpose. As the beloved pet of John Gray, a night watchman, Bobby was a constant presence in his master's life. Together, they patrolled the streets of Edinburgh, sharing quiet moments and building a bond that would leave an indelible mark on both their lives.

When John Gray passed away in 1858, he was laid to rest in Greyfriars Kirkyard, a cemetery nestled in the heart of Edinburgh. The loss of his master was a defining moment for Bobby, but instead of succumbing to despair, he transformed his grief into a daily act of devotion.

The Vigil Begins

Not long after John's burial, Bobby began his remarkable vigil. Each day, the little Skye Terrier made his way to Greyfriars Kirkyard, taking up residence near John's grave. Rain or shine, through Scotland's bitter winters and warm summers, Bobby's routine remained steadfast. His presence became a constant at the cemetery, a living testament to the bond he shared with his master.

Caretakers at the cemetery initially tried to discourage Bobby's visits, as dogs weren't typically allowed. However, Bobby's determination—and perhaps the sadness in his eyes—softened their hearts. They soon realized he wasn't just a stray; he was a dog with a purpose, guarding the resting place of the man he loved most.

Bobby's behavior touched those who witnessed it. His loyalty was more than an act of instinct; it was a profound expression of love that resonated with everyone who encountered him.

Adopted by a Community

As Bobby's vigil continued, the people of Edinburgh took notice. Far from being a nuisance, Bobby became a beloved figure in the city. Locals began leaving food and water for him, ensuring he had the sustenance needed to endure his long days at the cemetery.

One of Bobby's most ardent supporters was James Brown, a local restaurant owner who fed Bobby regularly. Brown's kindness became a cornerstone of Bobby's survival, and the bond between the two grew over the years. Others followed suit, offering support in small but meaningful ways. Bobby, once just a loyal dog, became a symbol of love and devotion for the entire community.

In 1867, Edinburgh's city council officially recognized Bobby's special role at Greyfriars Kirkyard. They even paid for his license, providing him with a brass-studded collar that signified his unique status. This small gesture not only legitimized Bobby's presence but also ensured his safety in a city where stray dogs were often unwelcome.

Enduring Through the Years

For 14 years, Bobby maintained his daily vigil, becoming as much a part of Greyfriars Kirkyard as the headstones and trees. His small frame, often curled near John Gray's grave, became a familiar and comforting sight for visitors.

Bobby endured harsh winters and torrential rains, but his determination never faltered. His resilience was a source of inspiration to those who followed his story. Locals and travelers alike marveled at his unshakable devotion, finding in Bobby's actions a reflection of their own capacity for love and loyalty.

Bobby's presence also brought a sense of peace to the cemetery. Though he couldn't speak, his actions communicated volumes, reminding people of the enduring nature of love even in the face of loss.

A Quiet Farewell

In January 1872, after 14 years of devotion, Greyfriars Bobby passed away. By then, he was an old dog, his muzzle grayed and his body slowed by the passage of time. But even as his life drew to a close, Bobby's spirit remained as loyal as ever.

Bobby was laid to rest near John Gray's grave, ensuring the two companions would remain together in death as they had been in life. His burial site, marked by a small memorial, quickly became a place of pilgrimage for those who had been moved by his story.

A Legacy of Love

Today, Bobby's legacy lives on. A bronze statue of him, erected in 1873 near the entrance to Greyfriars Kirkyard, stands as a tribute to his extraordinary loyalty. The statue, crafted with loving detail, captures Bobby's spirit and continues to draw visitors from around the world.

Greyfriars Bobby's story has been immortalized in books, films, and folklore, ensuring that his devotion will never be forgotten. His tale has become a timeless reminder of the deep connections that can exist between humans and their animal companions.

Lessons from Bobby's Vigil

Bobby's daily visits to Greyfriars Kirkyard hold profound lessons for us all. His actions demonstrate the enduring power of love and the resilience of the heart, even in the face of loss. Bobby's story encourages us to cherish the relationships in our lives, reminding us of the impact a single bond can have.

- **Unwavering Loyalty**: Bobby's 14-year vigil is a testament to the loyalty that defines the relationship between humans and their dogs. His dedication inspires us to value the commitments we make to those we love.
- **The Power of Community**: The way the people of Edinburgh rallied around Bobby shows the importance of compassion and support. Their kindness enabled him to carry out his remarkable vigil.
- **Love That Transcends Loss**: Bobby's devotion didn't end with John Gray's death. His story is a poignant reminder that love endures, even in the absence of the one we hold dear.

Greyfriars Bobby's daily vigil was more than just a routine; it was an extraordinary act of love that continues to inspire people today. His story reminds us of the unique bond between dogs and their owners, a bond that defies the limitations of time and space.

In his unwavering loyalty, Bobby left a legacy that endures in the hearts of those who hear his tale. His life may have been small in scale, but the impact of his devotion is immeasurable, proving that even the simplest acts of love can leave an everlasting mark on the world.

A Tale Immortalized: Statues, Books, and Films Celebrating Bobby's Loyalty

Greyfriars Bobby's extraordinary loyalty has captured the imagination of generations. From his daily vigil at Greyfriars Kirkyard to his touching bond with his late master, John Gray, Bobby's story has transcended time, becoming a symbol of love and devotion. This Skye Terrier, once a humble companion, has been immortalized through statues, books, films, and countless retellings.

The enduring appeal of Bobby's story lies in its universality. In a world often marked by change and uncertainty, his unwavering loyalty resonates deeply. This chapter explores how Bobby's legacy has been preserved, celebrated, and shared, ensuring his story continues to inspire people across the globe.

The Statue That Keeps Watch

One of the most enduring tributes to Greyfriars Bobby is the bronze statue that stands near the entrance to Greyfriars Kirkyard in Edinburgh. Erected in 1873, just a year after Bobby's death, the statue was commissioned by Baroness Angela Burdett-Coutts, a philanthropist moved by Bobby's story.

The statue, created by sculptor William Brodie, captures Bobby's likeness in exquisite detail. Perched atop a granite fountain, the little terrier gazes out with a look of quiet determination, as if still keeping watch over his master's grave. Beneath the statue is an inscription that reads, *"Greyfriars Bobby – Died 14th January 1872 – Aged 16 Years – Let His Loyalty and Devotion Be a Lesson to Us All."*

Over the years, the statue has become a beloved landmark, drawing visitors from around the world. Tourists and locals alike stop to take photos, leave flowers, or simply reflect on Bobby's extraordinary story. The statue serves as a tangible reminder of his loyalty, ensuring his memory remains alive in the heart of Edinburgh.

Immortalized in Print

Bobby's story has been told and retold in numerous books, each capturing the essence of his remarkable life. Perhaps the most famous literary tribute is *Greyfriars Bobby* by Eleanor Atkinson, published in 1912. Though fictionalized, Atkinson's novel brought Bobby's story to an international audience, highlighting his bond with John Gray and the kindness of the Edinburgh community.

Atkinson's portrayal of Bobby struck a chord with readers, turning him into a global symbol of loyalty. The book's success also inspired other authors to explore Bobby's story, leading to a rich collection of works that delve into his life from various perspectives.

Children's literature, in particular, has embraced Bobby's tale. Simplified retellings have introduced young readers to the values of love, loyalty, and devotion through the lens of Bobby's story. These books not only keep his legacy alive but also teach timeless lessons to new generations.

From Page to Screen

Greyfriars Bobby's journey didn't end with books; it made its way onto the silver screen, further solidifying his place in popular culture. One of the most notable adaptations is the 1961 Disney film *Greyfriars Bobby: The True Story of a Dog*.

The film, directed by Don Chaffey, dramatizes Bobby's life with a heartwarming narrative that emphasizes his bond with John Gray and the community that cared for him. While certain elements were fictionalized for cinematic appeal, the core of Bobby's story—his loyalty and love—remained intact.

Disney's portrayal introduced Bobby to audiences far beyond Edinburgh, bringing his tale to millions of viewers around the world. The film's success helped cement Bobby's status as a cultural icon and inspired other filmmakers to create adaptations and documentaries celebrating his life.

Beyond the Disney classic, Bobby's story has been featured in countless television programs and documentaries. These productions, ranging from historical explorations to heartfelt dramatizations, have ensured that his legacy continues to reach new audiences.

A Tale Retold Across Generations

Bobby's story has transcended its historical roots, becoming a universal narrative that resonates with people of all backgrounds. This universality has led to countless reinterpretations and retellings, each one adding a new layer to his legend.

Folklore and oral traditions have played a significant role in keeping Bobby's memory alive. In Edinburgh, locals often share his story with visitors, passing down the tale of his loyalty like a treasured heirloom. Tour guides at Greyfriars Kirkyard recount Bobby's vigil with a mix of reverence and pride, ensuring his spirit remains a vibrant part of the city's heritage.

Artists and illustrators have also contributed to Bobby's legacy. Paintings, sketches, and sculptures inspired by his story capture the emotions his tale evokes, from the sorrow of loss to the beauty of enduring love. These artistic tributes serve as another medium through which Bobby's loyalty is celebrated.

Inspiring Acts of Kindness

Bobby's story has not only inspired artistic and literary tributes but also sparked acts of kindness and compassion. His tale serves as a reminder of the importance of loyalty, love, and community, encouraging people to embrace these values in their own lives.

In Edinburgh, the story of Greyfriars Bobby has become a symbol of the city's character—a blend of history, heart, and humanity. For locals, Bobby is more than just a historical figure; he represents the best of what it means to care for others, whether human or animal.

Around the world, Bobby's story has inspired charitable initiatives and campaigns promoting animal welfare. His unwavering devotion highlights the unique bond between humans and their pets, motivating people to treat animals with kindness and respect.

A Legacy That Endures

More than a century after his passing, Greyfriars Bobby remains a symbol of love and loyalty. His story, immortalized through statues, books, and films, continues to resonate with people of all ages.

The enduring appeal of Bobby's tale lies in its simplicity. At its heart, it is the story of a dog who loved his master so deeply that even death could not sever their bond. This timeless narrative speaks to the universal longing for connection and the comfort that love provides, even in the face of loss.

Bobby's legacy reminds us that loyalty and devotion are not limited by time, place, or species. His actions, though small in scale, have left an immeasurable impact, inspiring generations to cherish the bonds they share with their loved ones.

A Lesson for All

Greyfriars Bobby's tale is more than a story; it is a lesson in love, loyalty, and the power of memory. His devotion to John Gray, celebrated in statues, books, and films, serves as a beacon of hope and inspiration.

As we reflect on Bobby's life, we are reminded of the profound connections that exist between humans and animals. These bonds, built on trust and love, enrich our lives and leave a lasting imprint on our hearts.

In celebrating Bobby's story, we honor not just the loyalty of one remarkable dog but also the enduring values that make life meaningful. His legacy is a testament to the power of love—a force that transcends time, place, and even death, leaving behind a tale that will be cherished for generations to come.

UNWAVERING LOYALTY: DOGS WHO CHANGED LIVES

***

Balto – The Sled Dog Who Saved a Town

The Call to Duty: How Balto Led a Team to Deliver Life-Saving Medicine to Nome, Alaska

In the icy wilderness of Alaska, where temperatures can plunge to life-threatening lows and blizzards rage with relentless fury, a small town faced a deadly outbreak that demanded a hero. That hero came in the form of Balto, a Siberian Husky whose courage and leadership became the stuff of legend. In the winter of 1925, Balto and his team of sled dogs braved the unforgiving Alaskan wilderness to deliver life-saving diphtheria antitoxin to the isolated town of Nome.

Balto's story is one of determination, teamwork, and the enduring bond between humans and their canine companions. His journey not only saved lives but also captured the hearts of millions, earning him a place in history as one of the most celebrated dogs of all time.

The Crisis in Nome

In January 1925, Nome, Alaska, a remote town with a population of fewer than 1,500 people, faced a dire situation. A diphtheria outbreak threatened to devastate the community, particularly its children. Diphtheria, a bacterial infection that attacks the respiratory system, was a death sentence without antitoxin, and Nome's limited supply was nearly exhausted.

The closest stockpile of diphtheria antitoxin was over 600 miles away in Anchorage. With no roads connecting the two towns and airplanes unable to fly due to extreme weather, the only viable solution was to transport the medicine via sled dog relay. The journey would be treacherous, involving frozen rivers, gale-force winds, and temperatures plummeting to -50°F (-45°C).

A Hero Steps Forward

The relay plan required 20 teams of sled dogs to transport the antitoxin in stages, covering a total distance of approximately 674 miles. Each musher and team would carry the serum through their designated section of the trail, battling the elements to ensure it reached Nome in time.

Balto, a Siberian Husky belonging to musher Gunnar Kaasen, was one of the dogs chosen for the final leg of the relay. Despite not being the fastest or most experienced sled dog, Balto had a reputation for reliability and determination. When the call to duty came, he rose to the occasion, leading his team into history.

Braving the Elements

Balto's leg of the journey was the most treacherous. By the time Kaasen and his team set out, the weather had deteriorated to near-blinding conditions. Snowstorms whipped across the trail, and visibility was reduced to almost nothing. Yet, Balto's instincts proved invaluable. He navigated the frozen terrain with remarkable precision, relying on his sense of smell and his unerring ability to find the safest path.

At one point, Kaasen nearly lost the precious cargo when the sled tipped over in the high winds. But Balto's steady leadership kept the team moving, ensuring they didn't falter under the intense pressure. Despite exhaustion and freezing conditions, Balto refused to stop, driven by a sense of duty that defied human understanding.

The most dangerous stretch of their route involved crossing the Topkok River, a frozen expanse that could give way underfoot at any moment. Balto's surefootedness and determination carried the team across, ensuring the serum remained safe.

A Triumph of Teamwork

On February 2, 1925, after traveling over 53 miles in brutal conditions, Balto and his team arrived in Nome with the antitoxin. Their delivery came just in time to prevent a full-scale epidemic, saving countless lives and averting a tragedy that would have devastated the small town.

While Balto is often credited as the hero, the success of the mission was a collective effort. The relay's completion depended on the courage of all the mushers and their dogs, who risked their lives to ensure the antitoxin reached Nome. Yet,

Balto's role in the final leg of the journey earned him widespread recognition, cementing his status as the face of this historic endeavor.

A Legacy of Bravery

News of the "Great Race of Mercy," as the relay came to be known, spread quickly. Balto became a national hero, celebrated for his bravery and determination. Statues were erected in his honor, most notably in Central Park, New York City, where a bronze likeness of Balto still stands today. The statue's inscription reads:

"Dedicated to the indomitable spirit of the sled dogs that relayed antitoxin 600 miles over rough ice, across treacherous waters, through Arctic blizzards from Nenana to the relief of stricken Nome in the Winter of 1925. Endurance · Fidelity · Intelligence."

Balto's fame also led to public appearances and even a starring role in a short film. While the attention brought recognition to the vital role sled dogs played in Arctic exploration and survival, it also raised awareness of the bond between humans and their canine companions—a bond built on trust, loyalty, and shared purpose.

The Forgotten Heroes

While Balto received much of the glory, other dogs and mushers played equally critical roles in the relay. Togo, another Siberian Husky, led a team that covered the longest and most grueling stretch of the journey, navigating over 260 miles through some of the harshest conditions. Togo's contributions were just as vital, and in recent years, efforts have been made to recognize his role in the mission.

Balto's fame, however, did not diminish the collective achievement of the relay. Together, the mushers and their dogs demonstrated what could be accomplished through teamwork, resilience, and an unwavering commitment to a shared goal.

Lessons from Balto's Journey

Balto's story offers more than a historical account of a remarkable event; it provides enduring lessons in courage, determination, and the power of teamwork. His journey reminds us that even in the face of overwhelming odds, the human-animal bond can achieve extraordinary outcomes.

For the people of Nome, the arrival of the antitoxin was more than just a medical victory—it was a testament to the strength of the human spirit and the unbreakable bond between sled dogs and their mushers. For the rest of the world, Balto's story became a symbol of hope and resilience, proving that heroes can come in all shapes and sizes—even with four paws and a wagging tail.

A Story Worth Remembering

Nearly a century after the Great Race of Mercy, Balto's story continues to inspire. His courage and determination, along with the bravery of all the sled dogs and mushers, remain a testament to the extraordinary lengths humans and animals will go to protect and care for one another.

Balto's statue in Central Park, the books and films celebrating his journey, and the annual commemorations of the relay all serve as reminders of this remarkable chapter in history. They keep alive the memory of a little Siberian Husky who, against all odds, answered the call to duty and delivered hope to a town in desperate need.

Endurance in the Arctic: The Harrowing Challenges Faced During the Serum Run

In the frozen wilderness of Alaska, survival requires strength, resilience, and an unyielding will to persevere. These qualities were tested to their limits during the historic 1925 serum run to Nome, a life-saving mission that spanned over 600 miles of harsh terrain and unforgiving Arctic weather. This daring relay, carried out by teams of sled dogs and their mushers, was a race against time to deliver diphtheria antitoxin to a town on the brink of disaster.

The serum run, also known as the "Great Race of Mercy," is remembered as a remarkable feat of human and animal endurance. Every leg of the journey was fraught with challenges that pushed the mushers and their dogs to the edge of their physical and mental capacities. From blistering cold and howling winds to treacherous ice and near-zero visibility, the Arctic threw its worst at them. Yet, their determination never wavered.

The Relentless Arctic Cold

The first and most daunting challenge faced during the serum run was the Arctic cold. Temperatures along the route often plunged below -50°F (-45°C), cold enough to freeze exposed skin in seconds. For the mushers, this meant constant vigilance to avoid frostbite and hypothermia. Layers of fur-lined parkas, mittens, and boots provided some protection, but nothing could fully shield them from the bone-chilling winds that cut through even the warmest clothing.

For the sled dogs, the cold was equally brutal. While Siberian Huskies and Alaskan Malamutes are bred for cold climates, the extreme temperatures still tested their limits. Ice and snow collected between their paw pads, and frost formed on their fur as they ran. The mushers regularly checked their dogs, removing ice and massaging their paws to ensure they could continue the journey.

Battling the Blinding Storms

One of the most harrowing aspects of the serum run was navigating through blinding snowstorms. These storms, driven by gale-force winds, reduced visibility to almost nothing, making it nearly impossible to see the trail ahead. Mushers relied on their dogs' instincts to find the path, trusting their lead dogs to guide the team through the whiteout conditions.

For some mushers, the storms brought moments of sheer terror. Crossing frozen rivers and lakes during a blizzard was particularly dangerous, as the ice could be thin in places and difficult to detect. A wrong step could mean plunging into icy waters, an outcome that would almost certainly result in death in such extreme conditions.

Despite the risks, the mushers and their teams pressed on. They knew that stopping for too long could mean succumbing to the cold or losing precious time in their race to save lives. Their perseverance in the face of these storms remains a testament to their courage and determination.

Navigating Treacherous Terrain

The trail from Nenana to Nome was a gauntlet of natural obstacles. The teams had to traverse frozen rivers, dense forests, open tundra, and mountain passes, each presenting its own unique challenges. The frozen Yukon River, one of the longest stretches of the route, was particularly perilous. The river's surface, though covered in ice, could crack and shift under the weight of the sleds, creating a constant threat of breaking through.

The most notorious section of the trail was the Topkok River and Norton Sound, where fierce winds and icy conditions made travel nearly impossible. Norton Sound, in particular, was a dangerous shortcut across open ice. While it shaved miles off the journey, the crossing was fraught with risk. Strong winds could blow teams off course, and the ice could give way at any moment. Yet, several mushers braved this path to save time, knowing that every second counted.

Exhaustion and Fatigue

The physical and mental toll of the serum run on both mushers and dogs was immense. The relay required them to push themselves to the limit, running for hours on end with little rest. Mushers often went without sleep, their eyes fixed on the trail as they guided their teams through the darkness and cold.

The dogs, though incredibly resilient, were not immune to exhaustion. Running for miles in extreme conditions required immense stamina and strength. Mushers cared for their teams with deep affection, pausing whenever possible to feed them, massage their muscles, and offer words of encouragement. The bond between mushers and their dogs was crucial, providing the mutual trust and support needed to keep going.

For Gunnar Kaasen and his lead dog, Balto, the final leg of the journey was particularly grueling. Already weary from days of travel, they faced some of the worst weather conditions of the entire run. Yet, their determination to deliver the serum to Nome propelled them forward, overcoming exhaustion and adversity to complete their mission.

The Pressure of Time

Perhaps the greatest challenge of the serum run was the relentless pressure of time. With the lives of Nome's residents hanging in the balance, every minute counted. The antitoxin had to be delivered before the outbreak spiraled out of control, making delays unthinkable.

The relay's tight schedule left no room for error. Each musher had to complete their leg of the journey as quickly as possible, passing the serum to the next team without delay. This urgency added to the already immense physical and mental strain, driving the mushers and their dogs to push beyond their limits.

Despite these challenges, the relay succeeded in delivering the antitoxin to Nome in just five and a half days—a feat that seemed almost impossible given the conditions. Their ability to rise to the occasion is a testament to the extraordinary determination of everyone involved.

A Triumph of the Human-Animal Bond

The success of the serum run was not only a triumph of endurance and bravery but also a celebration of the unique bond between humans and their canine companions. The mushers and their dogs worked as a team, relying on each other for strength and support. This bond was especially evident in the lead dogs, who guided their teams with unerring skill and unwavering loyalty.

Balto, Togo, and the other lead dogs became symbols of this remarkable partnership. Their ability to navigate the treacherous trail, even in the worst conditions, highlighted the incredible intelligence and dedication of sled dogs. The mushers, in turn, showed deep respect and care for their teams, recognizing their vital role in the mission's success.

Endurance That Inspires

The harrowing challenges faced during the serum run were unlike anything most people will ever experience. Yet, the story of this incredible journey continues to inspire. It serves as a reminder of the resilience of the human spirit, the strength of teamwork, and the enduring bond between humans and animals.

The Great Race of Mercy is not just a historical event; it is a testament to what can be achieved when determination and compassion unite. The mushers and their sled dogs braved the Arctic's worst conditions to save lives, proving that even in the face of overwhelming adversity, courage and perseverance can prevail.

Their legacy lives on, a beacon of hope and inspiration for

generations to come.

***

A Hero Remembered: Balto's Legacy as a Symbol of Courage and Loyalty

Balto, a name synonymous with bravery and loyalty, stands as one of the most celebrated dogs in history. His role in the 1925 serum run to Nome, Alaska, not only saved lives but also immortalized him as a symbol of courage and determination. Nearly a century later, Balto's story continues to inspire, serving as a reminder of the unbreakable bond between humans and animals.

From his leadership in the grueling final stretch of the serum run to his posthumous honors, Balto's legacy transcends time. This chapter delves into the enduring impact of Balto's life and explores how his story has become a beacon of hope and resilience.

The Serum Run: A Defining Moment

Balto's journey to fame began during the 1925 diphtheria outbreak in Nome, Alaska. With the town's children in grave danger and no means of quickly transporting antitoxin by air or sea, a sled dog relay became the only option. Over 20 mushers and their teams braved extreme weather and unforgiving terrain to deliver the life-saving serum, and it was Balto who led the final leg of the journey.

Under the guidance of musher Gunnar Kaasen, Balto navigated 53 miles of brutal conditions, including blizzards and near-zero visibility. His instincts, stamina, and unwavering determination ensured the serum arrived in Nome in time, saving countless lives. While the relay was a collective effort, Balto's role in the final leg earned him widespread recognition as the face of this historic event.

The Hero's Welcome

News of the serum run spread quickly, and Balto became an overnight sensation. He and Gunnar Kaasen were celebrated across the United States, with parades, public appearances, and widespread media coverage. Balto's story captured the hearts of people from all walks of life, embodying the values of courage, loyalty, and teamwork.

In 1925, a statue of Balto was unveiled in Central Park, New York City. Sculpted by Frederick George Richard Roth, the bronze statue honors Balto and all the sled dogs who participated in the relay. Its inscription reads:

"Dedicated to the indomitable spirit of the sled dogs that relayed antitoxin 600 miles over rough ice, across treacherous waters, through Arctic blizzards from Nenana to the relief of stricken Nome in the Winter of 1925. Endurance · Fidelity · Intelligence."

This statue remains a beloved landmark, visited by millions who continue to be moved by Balto's story.

Balto's Life After Fame

After the serum run, Balto and his team were taken on a tour of the United States. They made public appearances, delighting audiences and raising awareness about the heroics of sled dogs. However, fame came with its challenges. Balto and his team were eventually sold to a vaudeville promoter and ended up in less-than-ideal conditions, confined to a small, poorly maintained space in a dime museum in Los Angeles.

It was only through the efforts of Cleveland businessman George Kimble and a group of concerned citizens that Balto's fortunes changed. They raised enough money to purchase Balto and his team, bringing them to Cleveland, Ohio, where they lived out their days in the Cleveland Zoo. Here, Balto was cared for and loved, spending his later years in comfort.

A Legacy Preserved

Even after his death in 1933, Balto's legacy endured. His remains were preserved and mounted, and today they are on display at the Cleveland Museum of Natural History. Visitors from around the world come to see Balto, paying homage to a dog whose courage and loyalty saved lives and inspired millions.

Balto's story has also been immortalized in books, films, and educational programs. The 1995 animated movie *Balto* introduced his tale to a new generation, blending fact with fiction to highlight his heroic journey. While some artistic liberties were taken, the film captured the essence of Balto's bravery and the incredible bond between sled dogs and their mushers.

Inspiring Generations

Balto's legacy extends far beyond his role in the serum run. He has become a symbol of the resilience and loyalty that define the human-animal bond. His story resonates with people facing challenges, reminding them of the power of perseverance and teamwork.

For dog lovers, Balto represents the best qualities of canine companionship: unyielding devotion, courage in the face of danger, and an unwavering commitment to those they love. For historians and adventurers, his tale is a testament to the ingenuity and grit required to survive and thrive in extreme conditions.

Balto's Broader Impact

The attention generated by Balto's story also brought greater awareness to the vital role of sled dogs in Arctic and sub-Arctic regions. These dogs were not just companions but lifelines for many communities, serving as transportation, hauling supplies, and even delivering mail across vast, frozen landscapes.

Balto's fame helped shine a spotlight on this critical partnership, leading to increased respect and appreciation for sled dogs and their mushers. It also inspired the creation of events like the Iditarod Trail Sled Dog Race, which commemorates the spirit of the serum run and honors the legacy of dogs like Balto and Togo.

A Tale of Teamwork

While Balto is often celebrated as the hero of the serum run, it is important to acknowledge the collective effort of all the mushers and sled dogs involved. Each team faced their own unique challenges, from crossing frozen rivers to battling blizzards, and their contributions were equally vital to the mission's success.

Balto's story reminds us that heroes rarely act alone. His accomplishments were made possible by the trust and collaboration between him, his fellow dogs, and his musher, Gunnar Kaasen. Together, they achieved something extraordinary, proving that teamwork can overcome even the greatest obstacles.

Why Balto's Story Matters Today

In a world that often feels divided, Balto's story serves as a reminder of the power of unity, loyalty, and compassion. His courage in the face of overwhelming odds inspires us to rise to our own challenges, while his unwavering loyalty reminds us of the importance of standing by those we care about.

Balto's legacy is more than just a historical account; it is a celebration of the values that make us human. It teaches us that heroism comes in many forms and that even the smallest acts of bravery and kindness can leave a lasting impact.

Conclusion: A Hero for All Time

Nearly a century after his incredible journey, Balto remains a symbol of courage and loyalty. His story continues to be told, inspiring new generations to believe in the power of perseverance and the strength of the human-animal bond.

As we reflect on Balto's legacy, we are reminded that heroes can come in all shapes and sizes—even with four paws and a wagging tail. Balto's life may have ended long ago, but his spirit lives on, a shining example of what it means to be truly heroic.

UNWAVERING LOYALTY: DOGS WHO CHANGED LIVES

BALTO

***

What Dogs Teach Us About Loyalty

Timeless Lessons: Exploring How These Stories Reflect the Values of Loyalty and Devotion

In a world that often feels chaotic and unpredictable, the stories of loyal dogs like Hachiko, Capitan, Balto, and others offer a grounding reminder of values that never go out of style. Their tales of unwavering devotion resonate deeply with us because they reflect ideals we hold dear: loyalty, love, perseverance, and selflessness. These dogs, through their actions, have become silent teachers, imparting lessons that transcend cultures, generations, and species.

As we reflect on their stories, we are invited to think about what it means to truly dedicate ourselves to someone or something. These timeless lessons, drawn from the lives of our canine heroes, can inspire us to lead lives rooted in connection, commitment, and compassion.

Loyalty as a Cornerstone of Relationships

The defining thread in all these stories is loyalty—a quality that we instinctively admire. Whether it's Hachiko waiting at Shibuya Station for his master's return or Capitan standing guard at his owner's grave for over a decade, these dogs exemplify a devotion that remains steadfast, even in the face of loss.

For Hachiko, loyalty wasn't simply an act but a way of being. Every day for nine years, he returned to the station, hoping to reunite with his beloved master. This profound consistency teaches us that loyalty isn't about convenience or reward; it's about commitment.

Similarly, Capitan's daily vigil at his owner's grave speaks to a bond that transcends even death. His story reminds us that loyalty is not limited to physical presence but extends to emotional and spiritual dedication. These examples challenge us to consider the depth of our own commitments—to our loved ones, our communities, and our values.

Perseverance in the Face of Adversity

Another powerful lesson from these stories is the value of perseverance. The journey of Balto and the other sled dogs during the serum run, for example, highlights what it means to push forward despite seemingly insurmountable challenges. Battling Arctic blizzards, dangerous terrain, and sheer exhaustion, these dogs and their mushers demonstrated an unyielding determination to save lives.

This perseverance reflects a truth we all experience: life is not without obstacles. Yet, these stories remind us that resilience and a steadfast commitment to a purpose can carry us through even the most difficult times. Balto's endurance, both physical and mental, inspires us to face our own challenges with courage and grit.

Selflessness: The Heart of True Devotion

One of the most touching aspects of these stories is the selflessness of the dogs involved. They ask for nothing in return, giving their loyalty and love unconditionally. Their actions are not motivated by recognition or reward but by a pure connection to their human companions.

Greyfriars Bobby's unwavering dedication to his owner's memory is a poignant example of this selflessness. For 14 years, he remained at his owner's grave, embodying a devotion that was entirely altruistic. Bobby's story invites us to reflect on our own relationships and consider how we can show up for others without expecting anything in return.

This selflessness is also evident in the story of Bobbie the Wonder Dog, who traveled over 2,500 miles to reunite with his family. His incredible journey, driven solely by love and a desire to be with his humans, exemplifies the kind of devotion that transcends personal comfort and safety.

The Universal Language of Love

One of the most beautiful aspects of these stories is how they illustrate the universal language of love. Dogs, with their limited ability to communicate verbally, rely on actions to express their feelings. Through their loyalty, perseverance, and devotion, they remind us that love doesn't always need words—it is felt and shown through consistent, meaningful acts.

Hachiko's daily presence at the station was an act of love, a silent declaration of his bond with his master. Similarly, the actions of Balto and his team during the serum run were driven by a love for their human partners and a shared sense of purpose. These examples show us that love is about showing up, especially in times of need, and that our actions often speak louder than words.

Lessons in Community and Connection

These stories also highlight the importance of community and the role it plays in sustaining acts of devotion. Capitan's tale is particularly illustrative of this. While he remained at his owner's grave, the local community stepped in to care for him, providing food and shelter. Their actions underscored the power of collective kindness and the interconnectedness of all living beings.

Balto's story, too, reflects the spirit of community. The serum run was not a solo effort but a collaborative mission involving multiple teams of sled dogs and mushers. Their success depended on trust, teamwork, and a shared commitment to a greater cause. These stories remind us that while individual acts of loyalty and bravery are inspiring, they are often supported and amplified by the strength of the community around them.

Inspiration for Our Own Lives

The stories of these remarkable dogs offer more than admiration; they inspire us to embody similar values in our own lives. Loyalty, perseverance, selflessness, and love are qualities that we can strive to cultivate in our relationships and endeavors.

These lessons are particularly relevant in today's fast-paced, often disconnected world. In a time when commitments can feel fleeting and relationships strained, the unwavering devotion of these dogs serves as a powerful example of what it means to truly care for and stand by others.

The Enduring Power of Storytelling

One of the reasons these stories continue to resonate is their timeless appeal. They remind us of universal truths that are as relevant today as they were decades ago. By sharing and celebrating these tales, we ensure that their lessons live on, inspiring future generations to value loyalty, compassion, and connection.

Balto, Hachiko, Capitan, and their fellow canine heroes are more than historical figures; they are symbols of the best in all of us. Their stories invite us to reflect, to strive, and to remember that even in the smallest of actions, we can make a meaningful impact.

Conclusion: Lessons to Carry Forward

The tales of these loyal dogs are not just heartwarming anecdotes; they are profound reminders of the qualities that make life meaningful. Loyalty, devotion, perseverance, selflessness, and love—these values, so beautifully embodied by our canine companions, are lessons we can carry forward in our own lives.

As we honor these remarkable animals, let us also take a moment to reflect on how we can emulate their virtues. Whether it's through deepening our commitments, showing kindness to others, or persevering through challenges, we, too, can strive to live with the same unwavering spirit.

In their quiet, unassuming way, these dogs have left a legacy that will endure for generations. Their stories remind us that even in a world of uncertainty, there are values that remain timeless—and that in loyalty and love, we find our greatest strength.

WHAT DOGS TEACH US ABOUT LOYALTY

***

Human-Animal Bond: Insights into Why Dogs Exhibit Such Extraordinary Commitment

The bond between humans and dogs is one of the most profound relationships in the natural world. For thousands of years, dogs have been our companions, protectors, and helpers, forging a unique connection that goes beyond mere coexistence. Their extraordinary commitment to humans—expressed through acts of loyalty, courage, and devotion—continues to amaze and inspire us.

But what drives this unwavering allegiance? Is it instinct, training, or something deeper? This chapter explores the origins and psychology of the human-dog bond, shedding light on why dogs demonstrate such extraordinary commitment and what we, as their human counterparts, can learn from it.

A Partnership Forged in History

The story of the human-dog bond began over 15,000 years ago when wolves, the ancestors of modern dogs, started associating with human groups. These early interactions were mutually beneficial: humans provided food scraps, while wolves offered protection and hunting assistance. Over time, selective breeding transformed wolves into domesticated dogs, whose temperaments and behaviors were better suited for companionship.

This co-evolution created a deep connection rooted in mutual dependence. Dogs evolved to read human emotions and respond to our needs, while humans grew to rely on dogs for their loyalty, intuition, and unique skills. This shared history laid the foundation for the extraordinary bond we see today, where dogs and humans not only coexist but thrive together.

The Psychology of Canine Loyalty

Dogs' commitment to their humans is often described as instinctual, but it is also influenced by emotional and social factors. At the core of this loyalty are a few key psychological and biological elements:

- **Pack Mentality:**
- Dogs are pack animals by nature. In the wild, a pack is essential for survival, providing safety, social structure, and resources. When a dog joins a human household, it instinctively perceives the family as its pack. This leads to behaviors that prioritize group harmony and protection, often manifesting as loyalty to the "alpha" figure or primary caregiver.
- **Oxytocin and Emotional Bonding:**
- Research shows that interactions between humans and dogs, such as petting, playing, or simply making eye contact, trigger the release of oxytocin, often called the "love hormone." This chemical strengthens the emotional bond between dogs and their owners, fostering trust and affection on both sides.
- **Empathy and Emotional Intelligence:**
- Dogs are remarkably attuned to human emotions. They can sense changes in tone, body language, and even pheromones, allowing them to respond to our moods and needs. This empathy deepens their connection with us, making their loyalty feel even more personal and heartfelt.

The Role of Training and Socialization

While some of a dog's loyalty is innate, training and socialization play a significant role in shaping their behavior. From an early age, dogs learn to associate humans with safety, nourishment, and companionship. Positive reinforcement techniques, where good behavior is rewarded with treats or praise, strengthen this bond, teaching dogs that staying close to their humans brings joy and security.

Socialization also exposes dogs to a variety of environments, people, and situations, helping them develop trust and adaptability. Dogs raised in loving, consistent environments are more likely to exhibit unwavering loyalty because they feel secure in their relationships.

The Power of Shared Experiences

One of the most profound aspects of the human-dog bond is how it is reinforced through shared experiences. Adventures, routines, and even quiet moments create a sense of togetherness that deepens the connection between dogs and their owners.

- **Routine and Rituals:**
- Dogs thrive on routine, finding comfort in predictable patterns. Whether it's a daily walk, mealtime, or a shared spot on the couch, these rituals create a sense of belonging and mutual reliance.
- **Overcoming Challenges Together:**
- When humans and dogs face challenges—such as navigating a difficult hike, coping with illness, or surviving a crisis—their bond strengthens. These shared struggles reinforce

trust and loyalty, as both parties rely on each other for support and guidance.
- **Expressions of Affection:**
- Simple acts, like scratching a dog's ears or offering a comforting word, go a long way in building emotional connections. Dogs recognize and respond to these gestures, reinforcing their commitment to their humans.

Why Dogs Go Above and Beyond

Dogs' extraordinary acts of loyalty, such as Hachiko's daily vigil or Balto's life-saving serum run, are not just driven by training or instinct. These behaviors often stem from their profound emotional connection to humans.

- **Unconditional Love:**
- Unlike humans, who may weigh costs and benefits, dogs love unconditionally. This pure, selfless affection drives them to act in ways that prioritize their humans' well-being, even at great personal risk.
- **Innate Protective Instincts:**
- Dogs' protective instincts are deeply rooted in their evolutionary history. Whether it's guarding their owners from danger or providing emotional support during tough times, their actions often reflect a strong desire to keep their humans safe.
- **A Sense of Purpose:**
- Dogs thrive when they have a purpose. Whether it's herding sheep, guiding the visually impaired, or simply being a loving companion, fulfilling a role that benefits their human companions reinforces their sense of loyalty

and satisfaction.

Lessons Humans Can Learn from Dogs

The loyalty and devotion dogs show to their humans offer valuable lessons for our own lives:

- **Be Present:**
- Dogs live in the moment, offering their undivided attention and love. They remind us to be present for the people we care about, cherishing each moment together.
- **Love Unconditionally:**
- Dogs don't hold grudges or place conditions on their affection. Their selfless love encourages us to approach our relationships with more forgiveness and generosity.
- **Commit to Your Pack:**
- Whether it's family, friends, or a community, dogs teach us the importance of loyalty and commitment to those who matter most.
- **Persevere Through Challenges:**
- Like Balto braving Arctic storms or Bobbie crossing 2,500 miles to reunite with his family, dogs show us the power of perseverance in achieving meaningful goals.

Why This Bond Matters

In a world that often feels disconnected, the human-dog bond serves as a reminder of what it means to truly care for and rely on one another. This relationship is a testament to the power of trust, empathy, and mutual support, values that are just as important in our interactions with fellow humans.

The stories of loyal dogs remind us of the extraordinary connections we can create when we open our hearts. They challenge us to be better companions, more compassionate caregivers, and unwavering supporters of those we love.

Conclusion: A Bond for the Ages

The human-animal bond is more than a relationship—it's a partnership built on trust, love, and shared purpose. Dogs, with their boundless loyalty and devotion, embody the best qualities of companionship, reminding us of what it means to truly connect.

As we celebrate these remarkable animals, let us also strive to nurture the values they teach us: loyalty, kindness, and a commitment to those who depend on us. In doing so, we honor the extraordinary bond that has shaped our lives for thousands of years—and will continue to inspire generations to come.

UNWAVERING LOYALTY: DOGS WHO CHANGED LIVES

✳✳✳

Living with Gratitude: How We Can Honor Dogs' Loyalty in Our Own Lives

Dogs have a way of showing us what unconditional love and loyalty truly mean. Their devotion is unwavering, their presence comforting, and their actions selfless. From the smallest gestures of affection to extraordinary acts of courage, dogs remind us daily of the beauty of commitment and trust.

But their loyalty is a gift, and gifts deserve acknowledgment. Living with gratitude for the dogs in our lives—not just through words but also through actions—honors their incredible devotion. In this chapter, we'll explore how we can recognize and celebrate the loyalty of our canine companions and integrate those lessons into our own lives.

1. Recognizing the Unique Bond

The first step in honoring dogs' loyalty is acknowledging the uniqueness of the bond we share with them. Dogs aren't just pets; they're family, confidants, and often our greatest sources of emotional support. Recognizing their role in our lives helps us approach our relationship with a sense of gratitude and respect.

- **Appreciating the Small Moments:**
- Every wag of the tail, warm nuzzle, or excited greeting is a display of love. Taking a moment to cherish these everyday acts helps us stay grounded in the present and value their companionship.
- **Acknowledging Their Emotional Intelligence:**

- Dogs can sense when we're sad, stressed, or joyful, and they respond accordingly. Their empathy is a gift, reminding us of the importance of emotional connections.
- **Understanding Their Perspective:**
- Dogs live in the moment and find joy in the simplest things. By embracing their perspective, we can learn to focus less on worries and more on the joys of life.

2. Acts of Gratitude in Everyday Life

Gratitude isn't just about feeling thankful; it's about showing it. Honoring dogs' loyalty means meeting their needs with the same consistency and care they show us.

- **Providing Consistent Care:**
- A dog's loyalty deserves reciprocation through attentive care. This includes regular vet visits, nutritious food, and plenty of exercise. By prioritizing their well-being, we show that their health and happiness matter to us.
- **Offering Quality Time:**
- Dogs thrive on attention and companionship. Setting aside dedicated time to play, walk, or simply cuddle with them strengthens the bond and assures them of their importance in our lives.
- **Being Patient and Understanding:**
- Just as they forgive our mistakes, we should extend patience to them. Whether they're learning a new command or adjusting to changes in their environment, our understanding reinforces the trust they place in us.

3. Learning from Their Loyalty

Dogs have an incredible ability to love unconditionally, forgive quickly, and live with unwavering devotion. By emulating these traits, we can honor their loyalty and improve our own lives.

- **Practicing Unconditional Love:**
- Dogs love us regardless of our flaws, bad days, or mistakes. Embracing this unconditional love in our relationships can deepen our connections with others.
- **Showing Forgiveness:**
- Dogs forgive instantly—whether it's an accidental step on their paw or a late dinner. Their ability to let go of grudges teaches us the importance of forgiveness in fostering healthy relationships.
- **Living with Purpose:**
- Whether it's protecting their family, assisting as service animals, or simply being a loyal companion, dogs find fulfillment in serving others. Their sense of purpose inspires us to seek meaning in our own actions and relationships.

4. Honoring Dogs Through Advocacy

Another way to honor dogs' loyalty is by advocating for their well-being. Countless dogs around the world suffer from neglect, abuse, or homelessness. Supporting causes that improve their lives is a powerful way to express our gratitude.

- **Adopting or Supporting Shelters:**
- By adopting rescue dogs or donating to animal shelters, we can give back to the species that gives us so much.

Volunteering time or resources helps ensure that more dogs receive the love and care they deserve.
- **Promoting Responsible Ownership:**
- Educating others about the responsibilities of pet ownership fosters a culture of care and respect for dogs. Simple acts, like sharing knowledge about proper training or advocating for spaying and neutering, make a difference.
- **Raising Awareness:**
- Stories like those of Hachiko, Capitan, and Balto highlight the incredible loyalty of dogs. Sharing these tales with others helps inspire greater appreciation and respect for their contributions to our lives.

5. Creating a Legacy of Gratitude

Honoring a dog's loyalty isn't limited to their lifetime. Even after they're gone, their impact can inspire us to continue living with gratitude and compassion.

- **Memorializing Their Contributions:**
- Creating a tribute—whether it's a photo album, a memorial garden, or simply sharing their story—helps preserve their legacy and reminds us of the love they gave unconditionally.
- **Paying It Forward:**
- In memory of a beloved dog, consider donating to a local shelter, sponsoring a service animal, or volunteering to help other dogs in need. This act of gratitude ensures their impact continues to ripple outward.
- **Living Their Lessons:**
- The best way to honor a dog's loyalty is by embodying the values they teach. Whether it's being present for loved ones,

showing kindness to strangers, or persevering through challenges, carrying their lessons forward is the ultimate tribute.

6. Gratitude as a Two-Way Street

The beauty of the human-dog bond lies in its reciprocity. While dogs are naturally loyal, they thrive on the love and care we give them. Gratitude enhances this bond, creating a relationship that benefits both sides.

- **Building Trust Through Gratitude:**
- When we respond to a dog's loyalty with appreciation and care, we deepen their trust in us. This mutual exchange of love and respect strengthens the bond and enriches both our lives.
- **Finding Joy in the Relationship:**
- Dogs remind us to find joy in the simple things—like a shared walk, a playful game, or a quiet moment together. By focusing on these moments, we cultivate gratitude not just for our dogs but for life itself.
- **Living with an Open Heart:**
- The gratitude we feel for dogs can extend to other areas of our lives. By appreciating their loyalty, we open ourselves to valuing the relationships, experiences, and opportunities that bring us happiness.

Conclusion: A Life Inspired by Loyalty

Dogs show us what it means to live with loyalty, love, and purpose. By honoring their devotion, we not only strengthen our bond with them but also enrich our own lives. Gratitude transforms this relationship into something even more profound—a partnership built on mutual care and respect.

As we reflect on the remarkable loyalty of dogs, let us strive to live with the same commitment, compassion, and presence they show us every day. In doing so, we honor their legacy and ensure that the lessons they teach continue to inspire us for generations to come.

WHAT DOGS TEACH US ABOUT LOYALTY

***

Conclusion: A Life Inspired by Loyalty

As we close this heartfelt journey through the extraordinary stories of canine devotion, one thing becomes abundantly clear: dogs embody the very best of what it means to be loyal, loving, and steadfast. From Hachiko's daily vigil at Shibuya Station to Balto's heroic trek through the Arctic, these remarkable tales remind us of the profound bond between humans and dogs—a relationship built on trust, commitment, and an unspoken understanding that transcends words.

These stories are not just about dogs; they are about us, too. They are mirrors reflecting the values we admire and aspire to live by. Loyalty, courage, resilience, and unconditional love—these traits, so vividly displayed by our canine companions, challenge us to be better in our own lives.

Dogs teach us to live in the moment, to find joy in the simplest gestures, and to remain steadfast in the face of adversity. They remind us that true loyalty requires showing up, day after day, with love in our hearts and a willingness to give our best. Whether it's a wagging tail greeting us at the door or a life-saving act of courage, dogs remind us that small, consistent actions can leave a lasting impact.

Carrying the Lessons Forward

The stories in this book are more than touching narratives; they are lessons. From Hachiko's enduring hope to Capitan's unwavering vigil, Bobbie's unyielding determination, Greyfriars Bobby's lifelong devotion, and Balto's courageous leadership, each story offers a unique perspective on what it means to be truly devoted.

We can carry these lessons forward in how we treat others—our families, friends, and communities. Dogs show us the value of being present, offering kindness without expectation, and standing by those we care about through thick and thin. By emulating these traits, we not only honor our canine companions but also enrich our relationships and create a ripple effect of positivity in the world.

Honoring the Bond

As we honor the loyalty of dogs, it's important to remember the reciprocal nature of this relationship. Dogs give so much, often asking for very little in return. By cherishing them, providing them with care and affection, and advocating for their well-being, we fulfill our part in this timeless partnership.

Their loyalty is not just a gift; it's a reminder to appreciate the love we receive and to give it freely in return. Through our actions, we can show gratitude for the countless ways dogs enrich our lives, from their quiet companionship to their heroic deeds.

A Legacy of Love

The bond between humans and dogs is one of life's greatest treasures. It has endured for thousands of years, evolving from a partnership of survival to a relationship of profound emotional depth. As we continue to share our lives with these remarkable animals, let us celebrate their loyalty not just with words but through how we live.

Let us carry their lessons into our relationships, embrace their unwavering spirit, and honor their legacy by striving to be as devoted, compassionate, and courageous as they are. In doing so, we ensure that the stories of loyalty and love, like those shared in this book, continue to inspire us for generations to come.

And so, we end this journey with a heartfelt thank you to our loyal companions—our dogs. They are not just animals; they are family, and their loyalty knows no bounds.

CONCLUSION: A LIFE INSPIRED BY LOYALTY

***

Tribute

TRIBUTE

SUMAN

BOOKS

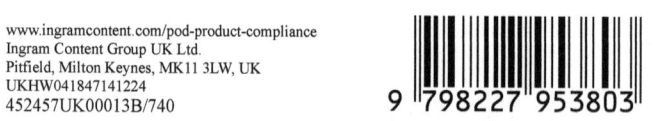